CATCHING FISH

CATCHING
FISH
Knowing their feeding habits

Richard Walker

DAVID & CHARLES

Newton Abbot   London   North Pomfret (Vt)

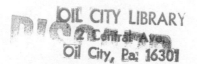

British Library Cataloguing in Publication Data

Walker, Richard
　Catching fish.
　1. Fishes — Food
　2. Fishing
　I. Title
　597'.053　　QL639.3

　ISBN 0-7153-8198-9

First published 1981
Second impression 1983

Printed in Great Britain
by Redwood Burn Limited Trowbridge Wiltshire
for David & Charles (Publishers) Limited
Brunel House　Newton Abbot　Devon

Published in the United States of America
by David & Charles Inc
North Pomfret　Vermont 05053　USA

Contents

Part Three: The Conditions

Preface

In the 1960s I wrote a little pamphlet called *How Fish Feed*, which was published at a very modest price. Owing to a change of policy by its publishers, it was quickly out of print, which I thought a pity, because what it said about the feeding behaviour of fish was, I believed, helpful to those wishing to catch them. Indeed, knowledge of this sort is a major factor in successful angling, since it indicates not only which baits are likely to be most successful but also where fish of different species are likely to be found; the conditions of weather, water temperature and light in which they feed best, and the nature of the bite-indications the angler may expect to see.

Angling demands greater knowledge of the quarry's feeding habits than any other field sport. You don't need to know what a pheasant eats in order to shoot it, or the diet of hares or foxes to pursue these animals with a pack of hounds. Angling, however, depends on whether you can persuade a fish to eat food, or what the fish thinks is food. If you can't, you don't catch! This is much more important than tackle choice or casting skill; the finest and most expensive tackle and the highest standard of skill are both useless unless you can put an acceptable bait, real or artificial, where the fish can and will take it.

In some cases it is necessary to know not only the nature of the food which various kinds of fish eat, but also the behaviour of the food itself, if it consists of live creatures of one sort or another. Winged insects, for example, are not often — though there are exceptions — found at the bottom of a river, lake or pond, whereas their larvae are. In fly fishing, knowledge of how insects and other creatures move is valuable, so that their artificial counterparts can be made to move in a similar manner.

Anglers of limited experience often express surprise at the ability of more capable fishermen to catch fish of particular

7

species 'to order'. 'How can you say you're going to catch perch?' they ask. 'After you've cast out, any sort of fish might take your bait!' That is in some measure true; the experienced, able angler does sometimes catch fish of different species from those he seeks, but in the foregoing example, he would reply: 'I've chosen a spot that probably holds perch because I know perch like to eat worms!'

So it is with other fishes; the angler who knows where, how, when and on what different sorts of fish feed, has a very great advantage.

Since *How Fish Feed* was published, I have had some twenty further years in which to learn more, both from my own experience, from fishing friends, and from readers of the angling press who have been kind enough to write and tell me about experiences. To these men I am indebted and I thank them sincerely.

I have also benefited from what science has found out, though I am rather less impressed by some scientific pronouncements than I used to be, having discovered not a few that were gravely mistaken. The behaviour of immature fish in laboratory tanks is seldom similar to that of mature fish in their natural environment. I therefore accept only such scientific pronouncements as seem probable in the light of angling experience, where fish behaviour is concerned. In other areas, however, scientific evidence is more valuable, as for example when it deals with light refraction, current effects, and other phenomena about which anglers should know.

For all these reasons, I have now been able to revise and add to the original small pamphlet, and also to add chapters about matters and species of fish that were not included in it.

The kindness and energy of Peter Maskell, to whom I am most grateful, have combined to select from my writings over many years some articles that are relevant to the subject, and I am glad he has done this because he is a far better judge of my work than I am myself. The articles appear as chapters, revised here and there, but I hope readers will forgive some inevitable repetition.

One aspect of the feeding of fish is seldom considered. This is the effect of changes due to human agencies. A power station using river water will raise the temperature for a considerable distance below its outfall, and thus not only encourage the proliferation of numerous items of fish-food, but also increase the number of days in each year during which the water is warm enough for fish to feed freely.

The leaching-in of various agricultural chemicals, herbicides, insecticides and fertilisers, can affect fish and fish-food very greatly; there is reason to believe that the volume of aquatic insect life has diminished considerably in the last twenty or thirty years. Other organisms, like crayfish, have vanished from some stretches of river. Borehole abstraction for water supply has reduced flows, so that rivers have become shallower and, in addition, reduced current speeds have caused more mud to be deposited, greatly changing the ecology, usually for the worse.

Sometimes, gross pollution kills fish, but much more common are the combined effects that reduce the numbers and size of the fish in our waters. There is little that anglers can do to combat these evils, beyond subscribing money to their representative bodies and to the Anglers' Co-operative Association, but this the majority adamantly refuses to do. 10 per cent of the cost of a single day's fishing is more, it seems, than anglers can afford to protect their own sport.

It would be inappropriate in this book to pursue that matter, however, and I therefore pass on to what I think is important to every angler; I can set out in this book what I have learned in the hope that it will help, but this can never be a complete substitute for an angler's own observations. I therefore strongly recommend every angler who wants to be successful to seek out a few waters that are sufficiently clear and shallow to allow the fish they hold to be seen easily. A great deal of what I know about how fish behave, how they feed and what they eat, was learned by watching the fish in such waters. If you know from watching them what they do when you can see them, you can guess much more accurately what they do when you can't. Thus it is well worth spending quite a lot of time watching fish instead of trying to catch them, to which end a hat with a broad brim, or a cap with a long wide peak, are of considerable assistance, as, of course, are polarised glasses.

There is an art in seeing fish. Don't look up at the sky or at brilliant reflections from the water's surface; if you do, the pupils of your eyes will shrink automatically and prevent you from seeing far into the depths. Don't just give an area of water a quick glance; stare into it for several minutes, categorising in your mind all its features. You will often find that fish that were at first invisible, appear as if by magic. For example, what at first seemed to be a pair of reddish-orange patches on the bottom suddenly becomes the pectoral fins of a barbel, and then you see more, and realise that you are looking at a whole shoal.

Or you may see nothing but a patch of water buttercup or, as some call it, streamer weed, waving in the current. Keep watching; out from under that weed swing a couple of chub, then back again. You'd have missed them if you hadn't spent several minutes watching. Don't hurry to try to catch fish you see like this. Watch a little longer to learn what they are doing. Then see how they react to free sample of bait. If you can find which baits they will take and which they won't, you're far more likely to succeed when you do start fishing, and, let me repeat, what you learn will stand you in good stead when you fish where the quarry can't be seen.

Richard Walker
Summer 1981

Part One:

The Basics

1 Temperature, current and other factors

The purpose of this book is to discuss the feeding of fresh-water fish, and I want to start by talking about the effects of temperature, current, oxygen, etc, on fish. I have often talked about temperature, because it is one of the most important factors. The body temperature of a fish is not kept steady as ours is. It rises and falls with the temperature of the water. As temperature falls, fish eat less and move less, and with nearly all species there is a temperature level below which fish won't feed at all and only move if they have to.

Very few kinds of fish are at all keen to feed when the temperature of the water falls below about 39 to 40°F (4°C). When temperatures are relatively high, fish are put off feed by lack of oxygen, because as water temperature rises, the amount of dissolved oxygen that water can hold falls. If there is hardly enough for the fish, they aren't keen to feed. They probably feel much as we do when we've been too long in a stuffy room.

So you see, for fish to feed freely, the water mustn't be too warm or too cold. The extremes between which fish will feed vary from one kind of fish to another. For example, chub will feed in a very wide range, whereas that of carp is quite narrow. Grayling will feed in water so cold that all other species are right off.

There are, however, other things that modify the effect of temperature. If fish have to use a lot of energy, they must feed to replace the loss, and for that reason, river fish will go on feeding at lower temperatures than lake fish, because they use more energy in contending with the current.

After severe floods have gone down a river, fish often feed well even in cold water. Such species as barbel and tench, that are not normally considered as winter fish, are frequently caught during or after heavy floods.

At the back-end of the coarse-fishing season, another effect comes into play. In many species, food is needed for the growth of spawn and fish that would have been right off feed at 45°F (7°C) in November will now feed at temperatures down to, and sometimes below, 40°F (4°C), even when the current has been moderate for several days.

In conditions that are suitable for the feeding of fish, it is still necessary for the fish to be conscious that food is available. There is strong evidence to show that very often, and with some kinds of fish nearly always, it is necessary for fish to see, or smell, quite a lot of food before they become interested in eating it. Furthermore, once their interest has been aroused by the presence of a lot of food of one kind, they are apt to ignore other kinds of food, not recognising it as food at all.

This has been described as preoccupation, a word which has appeared a good deal in angling writing in the last few years, and which will continue to appear a good deal in the future.

It is of immense importance to understand all this when we come to consider the effect of groundbaiting. It is very commonly thought that the purpose of groundbaiting is to attract fish. That is really only one of its effects for probably the most important is that of bringing fish on feed. In using it for this purpose, it has to be understood that bringing fish on feed with one sort of food can often make them hard, if not impossible, to catch with other baits for some considerable time.

There is another thing that seems to affect the feeding of fish, and that is light. I'm not going to pretend I know all about it, for I don't, and I don't think anyone else does, either. But in the last few seasons, I've had plenty of reason to think that the amount of light that reaches the fish plays a considerable part in deciding whether some kinds of fish will feed well or not. Other species don't seem much affected. For example, chub and rudd will feed in bright sunshine or complete darkness. But roach and tench don't seem to like too much light, while dace, perch and pike don't feed much if there is too little.

2 Casting light on a complex subject

Here are a few facts for those anglers who like thinking to think about. When a ray of light passes from air to water. it gets bent; this is called refraction. But not all light rays pass from air to water, because if they strike the surface at a small-enough angle they are reflected. They're reflected at any angle less than about 10°.

This is important to the angler for two reasons. The first is that if he keeps low enough, fish can't see him. Even if there is no cover at all, they still can't see him if he keeps the top of his head below a line that makes an angle of 10° to the surface. In practice, since you can't carry out measurements of angles and distances very easily, all you need remember is that you should keep as low as possible, and the nearer you are to the fish, the lower you have to keep to avoid being seen.

The second thing about this angle of reflection is that once the sun has sunk in the sky to the point where its direct rays make an angle of less than 10° to the water, those direct rays no longer penetrate the surface.

Depending upon the amount of reflected light from the sky, there will be a more or less rapid reduction of the amount of underwater light as the sun passes through this critical angle. With a clear sky and a calm surface on the water, it will only take a few minutes for an enormous reduction in underwater light to take place. A ripple or wave will extend the time during which the sharp drop in underwater light occurs; if there is much cloud about and the sun is obscured, obviously the drop in light will be much less.

I think it very likely that the well-known tendency of fish to start feeding, often quite suddenly, in the evening may be due to this sudden drop in underwater light. After it has happened, the fish can easily see anything on or above the surface, but anything on or above the surface will find it difficult if not impossible to see the fish.

Probably the process of evolution has selected fish whose instincts are to move and feed freely as soon as they notice this sharp drop in underwater illumination; at that time they are much safer from predators like herons, ospreys, fish-eagles and others. Don't tell me that the fish don't have to worry about ospreys and fish-eagles nowadays; their instincts were evolved when there were plenty of such birds around.

Experienced anglers will have noticed that the brighter and sunnier a day has been, the more suddenly and eagerly the fish begin to feed at this critical time, when the sun has dropped below an angle of 10° to the water. Trout fishers especially will know that the most frantic evening rise follows a sunny day, when the sun begins to look a bit reddish. Red light doesn't penetrate water so well as other colours anyway, and on the kind of day I am talking about the surface of the water usually becomes calm in the evening, so that the reduction of underwater light is pretty sudden.

That's when fish start walloping about all over the place — and that's often when they prove difficult to catch, for they can see the angler's leader all too easily.

I just remarked that red light doesn't penetrate water as well as other colours. In fact, what happens is that the various colours of the spectrum are eliminated as you go deeper and by the time you're down ten feet or so, all you have left is bluish-green, as any underwater swimmer will tell you. Consequently, it makes practically no difference what colour fly or spinner you use if you're fishing fairly deep, because they'll all appear in various shades of blue-green to black.

This works in another way; if you are fishing a fly or plug near the surface and a fish comes up from fairly deep water to have a look at it, its colours will appear brighter and brighter to the fish as it gets nearer and nearer. That may explain why sometimes a fish will come up at a fly or plug but turn away just before taking. It has seen a colour or colours that it doesn't like, but which were invisible to it when it was deeper down.

My car has windows of tinted glass of a very pale bluish-green. If I open a window, the white clouds all look pink, until my eyes have adapted themselves. Fish live in a world lit mainly by bluish-green light and they, no doubt, adapt exactly as we do. To some extent, all colours penetrate a few feet below the surface though there will be more light at the blue-green end of the spectrum than at the orange-red end. Fish whose eyes have adapted will therefore be able to see these other colours but as I have said, the closer to the surface the fish moves, the brighter these other colours will appear.

Until the fish adapts, they will appear temporarily brighter, redder, than they would have done had the fish been swimming close to the top all the time; whereas greens and blues will look, again temporarily, less bright.

This may have some importance to the fly fisher; I'll tell you why. Take an insect like the blue-winged olive. When this fly hatches, it looks to us as if it has a body the colour of a ripe greengage. What it really has is an orange-red body inside a blue skin. To a trout that comes up to take it, its translucent body probably appears orange. An artificial tied opaque yellowish-green body won't look orange to such a trout; which is perhaps why a well-known fly, the Orange Quill, which does have a bright-orange body, attracts trout when they are feeding on blue-winged olives.

Don't let anyone convince you that fish can't tell one colour from another. They can see all the colours we can see, and very likely some that we can't, like ultra-violet and infra-red.

But anglers differ about colours, don't they? I know some expert reservoir-trout fishers who say you should use a gaudy fly on a bright day and a drab fly on a dull day. I also know many salmon fishers who advise the direct opposite! Perhaps a little more thought about what fish can see may resolve the different opinions.

3 How fish get their food

I have described briefly the factors that decide whether fish will feed or not. From now on, I'm going to assume that the fish are feeding, and deal with what methods the different species use to get their food.

Fish fall into various groups from this point of view. The first group includes those fish that dig in the bottom for food. Carp, tench, barbel, gudgeon and loach all have barbules, or 'whiskers', which allow them to detect the presence of various creatures, like bloodworms, mayfly, nymphs, worms, etc, in the bottom mud or sand. They suck in mouthfuls of the bottom and sort out stuff they can swallow. Carp and tench swallow quite a lot of mud as well as the organisms it contains. Of course, these kinds of fish often get food without digging, but this is their main way of getting a living, so we can call this group the bottom diggers.

Next come the fish that get most of their food from the bottom, but not by digging in it. Instead, they pick up food lying on the bottom. Typical of this sort are roach and bream; also in this group come crucian carp, while dace and chub can be regarded as half in the group and half out of it. Let's call this group the bottom pickers. All their food isn't taken off the bottom, of course. Some is picked off weed, and some is brought down by the current.

Thirdly, we have what I call the opportunist feeders. Chub, perch and trout come into this group. None of these fish is fussy about how or where they get their food, nor, in spite of what we read about fastidious fish, do they care much what they eat. Trout and perch prefer meat to veg, whereas chub will eat practically anything. But all these fish will feed at the surface, at mid-water, or at the bottom.

Many anglers, when asked what they're fishing for, reply: 'Anything that comes along.' Chub, perch and trout work on the same basis in their feeding. They can become preoccupied with one particular food, like all other fish, at times. But they start off with entirely open minds about where and what they will eat.

Rudd and dace I am going to class as insect-eating surface feeders. I know that both species do a lot of bottom picking too, but to class them with the true bottom pickers would be a mistake, because when we come to fish for them, we have to take into full account their different habits.

Finally, we have pike, which are predatory scavengers. At one time it was thought that pike lived entirely on live fish. I think that pike will eat anything they can get that could be called animal matter. They eat live fish, dead fish, crayfish, birds, animals, insects, worms — anything they come across when in a feeding mood.

Now, you'll have realised by this point that my classifying of the various species is as full of loop-holes as an Act of Parliament, and I want to make it clear that there's nothing cut-and-dried about it. I've simply arranged the fish according to their main feeding habits — what they do most of the time in most waters. The angler, however, has always to be alive to the possibility of a fish, or fishes, deciding to feed in a manner which is not typical of the species.

For example, there is no more typical bottom feeder than the barbel. Yet I have seen a barbel of record size come up and take a slice of bread from the surface. Trout are not supposed to eat vegetable matter, yet I caught one once that had a bellyful of cooked broad beans. Rudd aren't commonly regarded as predatory fish, yet there are times when a small spoon or devon will catch one after another.

But by using angling methods suited to the various feeding habits of these different groups of fish, you can be more often right in your technique. And when fish move out of their right category and into another, why, you say to yourself: 'If these rudd are going to behave like tench today, then I must use tench-fishing tactics.'

19

Part Two:

The Fish

4 How barbel feed

The barbel has always been regarded as one of the most mysterious of our fish. While there are anglers who do catch barbel fairly consistently, no one really knows a great deal about their habits. Although barbel are sometimes found alone or in twos and threes, it is much more common to meet with them in good-sized shoals. They are, in fact, typical shoal fish and either feed or refuse to feed in a body.

When they are feeding naturally, which is almost always at the bottom, they dig among the stones for various small organisms, of which the river-bed holds many different kinds. Not only do they feel about under small stones with those sensitive barbules, they can and do lift up quite large stones to get at what's underneath. Their mouths are used like suckers for this purpose. This habit, which I have often observed, may give a clue to what they eat. On some waters, barbel suck the alga from the stones on which it grows. They seem to do it mainly after dark, and in the morning you can see patches of clean stones, usually circular and as big as a dustbin lid, where barbel have been feeding in this way. I believe they eat more things like crayfish, bullheads, loach and lampreys than is commonly believed, and that the use of any of these as baits might be very effective.

Lampreys, or pieces of lamprey, used to be considered a deadly barbel bait on the Thames, but they're hard to get nowadays. I think a loach or a crayfish might do quite as well, and either could easily be fished on tackle well able to handle a barbel of record size.

Barbel will also dig for such things as mayfly nymphs and various kinds of worms that live in sandy silt, and it is amazing how they can break up stiff balls of clay and get at worms inside. You need never worry about a worm bait burying itself in the bottom when after barbel. If they want it, they'll soon have it out.

Another thing which barbel eat, in common with most if not all members of the carp family, is silkweed, and they will sometimes feed on it in hot, bright conditions when they don't seem in the least interested in anything else.

Barbel will on occasion get down to methodical feeding like a herd of cows in a meadow, all working in one direction, generally upstream. But every so often you see one of the fish whip round, swim downstream, and then come up and rejoin the rear of the shoal.

Patrick Chalmers, in his book *At the Tail of the Weir*, said that barbel definitely take it in turns to have a go at a big clay pudding full of worms, each fish turning downstream when it's got a worm, and joining the end of the queue to wait for its next turn. I think there may be much truth in this, and that it explains the terrific thumping bite one often gets from barbel. When the leger is used, the bite nearly takes the rod out of your hand, and the way the fish moves when struck shows that it must have been headed downstream.

But barbel don't always head downstream when they've taken a bait, because every so often the indication of a bite is a sort of trembling of the rod top. It feels almost as if someone is filing away at the line. If you strike, sometimes you connect, sometimes not. If you wait, sometimes a solid pull develops, sometimes the trembling stops and you reel up to find the bait gone. What the fish are doing to cause this trembling, I don't quite know, but I suspect they're deliberately trying to break up the bait. I don't suggest they have the sense to know what a hook and line are, but they may feel the bait is tethered and try to get it clear.

From the angler's point of view, barbel can be persuaded to eat almost anything if water conditions are favourable to their feeding and enough of the food chosen for bait is put in correctly for groundbait. Put in enough bread-and-bran groundbait, and you can get the barbel refusing to touch paste, or flake, or cheese — all they'll take is bread-and-bran. And then bread-and-bran gets described as a wonderful bait for barbel!

24

For most species of coarse fish, attempting to use their natural food as bait is seldom very successful, because it is either hard to get, difficult to use as hook-bait, is in quantities too small to use as groundbait, or something of that sort. It has always seemed to me that barbel may be the exception to this, and that some of their natural foods may prove not only usable but very effective.

I must not forget to add that, although barbel will sometimes bite in sunny conditions, they seem to prefer to wait for a relatively low light strength before commencing serious feeding, and in summer, early morning or late evening are generally the best times to fish — as with so many coarse fishes. In my experience the middle of the night is by no means the best time. This may be because barbel often leave their daytime haunts once it has become dark, and move to other, usually shallower, places to feed. If one knew to which shallow the barbel intended to move advantage could be taken of this habit, but I have never been able to predict it. It might be only twenty or thirty yards from the swim where the barbel are in the daytime, or it might be as much as half-a-mile away, upstream or down.

Barbel also move from their usual daytime abodes if the current speeds up, or if the water becomes muddy or much coloured. In these conditions they tend to move into slower, shallower water close to the banks.

5 The barbel haunt under a shelf of rock

Once I fished a small stream that holds some barbel, something I had hoped to do for many years. If you want to learn about the habits of fish, you've got to be able to watch them and watching them isn't very easy in a river the size of the Thames. Even the Hampshire Avon doesn't let you watch fish very easily, clear though its water usually is.

At one point in the stream I was fishing there is a place where the water rushes over an outcrop of rock that forms a shelf, which the current has undermined. Because the stream is narrowest at that point, a wooden footbridge has been built, and you can stand on this and look down at the rocks. When the sun is shining, it is possible to see barbel moving about, coming out from under the shelf and then going back again.

I didn't find them myself. In fact, I would have expected them to be lower down, at the tail-end of the fast water caused by the narrowing of the stream and the rock shelf. But they weren't in the expected place; that was occupied by a number of chub of no great size.

A very observant and skilful angler, John Leonardi, pointed out the barbel right under the rock. It looked as though a very heavy lead would be needed to get down through the extremely fast water at the surface, and that was the method John adopted, fishing from the footbridge.

But on a later visit, I found to my surprise that by fishing from the bank just below the bridge, and casting in exactly the right place, it was possible to get right under the shelf with no more lead than a single swan shot. The small side eddy between the fast water and the bank is the secret. A bait dropped into its very centre goes right down under the rock shelf, provided you keep the rod point in such a position that the line goes into the water in the very centre of that eddy; you not only have to feed out some line after casting to allow the bait to go down, but at the same time steer the line so as to keep it in the right place. It isn't as easy as it sounds because the centre of the eddy doesn't stay in the same place. It wanders about and it is necessary to move your rod accordingly; if you don't, the current grabs the line and hauls the bait out of its proper place.

I can't say I managed very well, for only one barbel was hooked, a fish just under 4lb, but I was pleased to have learnt a bit more about the places barbel like and ways of extracting them from those places. J. W. Martin wrote about the preference barbel show for a hollowed-out shelf in a river-bed, and I know one or two weirs where barbel like to lie right under the white water that comes over the sill. I shall be on the look-out for such places in future, and it may be that they can be fished without too much lead thus allowing the bait to move about naturally. Of course, the place into which the bait has to be cast is also the spot where the groundbait must go in. I just used loose lobworms, and they went down beautifully to the fishes' location.

I am sure it is a great mistake to use leads or groundbait heavier than necessary. A heavy lead will often anchor the bait beautifully steady in the wrong place, when a lighter one would let the bait be carried to where the fish are. I cannot emphasise too strongly that although most anglers still think a leger is a tackle to be slung out and which lies still on the bottom, there is no need for it to be so and, in fishing especially, to fish it so is more often than not the wrong way to use it. A correctly used moving leger is a true searching tackle and can explore the bottom of a river more minutely than any float tackle.

6 How bream feed

Like the barbel, the bream is a typical shoal fish. In fact, members of a bream shoal seem to have the shoaling instinct more fully developed than any other kind of fish. This is specially noticeable in their feeding. When bream aren't feeding, you can have a bait right in the middle of a shoal, and not a fish will touch it, perhaps for hours. Then, suddenly, the fish begin to feed, and you can catch one after another, until, equally suddenly, they stop feeding and you get no more bites.

Bream eat insects, molluscs and a certain amount of algae, including silkweed, but from an angler's point of view what they eat is less important than how they eat it. They get their living by picking food off the bottom. Of course, there are times when bream, like other bottom-feeding species, will take food at mid-water and even at the surface, but these occasions are the exception rather than the rule.

Normally, a feeding bream tilts its head downwards and, bringing its lips close to whatever it is it wants to pick up, it opens them and sucks. That applies when the food is on the bottom. But bream also get food by blowing as well as sucking. Many small organisms live just under the surface of the bottom mud, and bream will set this fine mud moving by blowing a jet of water at it. Anything edible is washed out and sucked in by the fish. I suppose this is really a form of bottom digging, but of course bream are quite incapable of digging into the bottom like tench and carp.

Methods of feeding such as this inevitably result in the fish often taking into its mouth stuff that it doesn't want to swallow, as well as what it does, and this gives rise to a habit of bream that it is important for anglers to know about. Bream wash their food. They do it by alternately sucking and blowing. Anyone who would like to see it being done can go and watch the bream in the aquarium at the London Zoo.

28

They up-end, suck in a mixture of food and fine sand from the bottom, rise up a few inches tail first, then blow out the mouthful and suck in the bit of bread, or whatever it is they're trying to get. They often suck it in and blow it out five or six times before they get it without too many sand particles.

It is very interesting to work out what will be the effect of such habits on a float, when a bream is at the bait. Of course, this sort of thing is likely to happen more with small baits and with baits that are fished on tackle that the fish can easily feel. One can imagine a bream never being willing to move off with a bait fished on lift tackle, with a single shot within an inch of the hook. I can never do much good with lift tackle for bream — but having said that, I expect to hear from plenty of readers who have!

With very big baits, bream whittle away and try to break them up. They'll peck away for hours at a tangerine-size lump of paste, until they've worked it down small enough to take into their mouths. A medium-sized bait (relative to the size of the fish) like a lobworm for a five-pounder, is the most likely size to be taken without messing about, especially if it happens to be fished on a firm bottom, where there is little loose stuff to be sucked in along with the bait.

You will have realised by now how typical bream bubbles are made. Gas in the bottom is, of course, sucked in by the fish and let out through the gill covers, and some is disturbed and floats up direct. The bream has, however, a very small mouth relative to its size, and individual fish don't release a lot of bubbles, though the amount produced by a shoal is considerable. Very often, the feeding of a bream shoal stirs up a lot of mud, as well as bubbles, and in many waters it is possible to locate these feeding shoals by watching for the discoloration they cause by mud-stirring. This has been remarked upon by most angling writers, but many anglers seem to expect to find as much discoloration as if cows were paddling in the water. This can in fact be seen in waters that are relatively small, shallow and either still or slow running, but in wide, deep rivers like the Thames, Ouse, or Witham, all that can be seen as a rule is a faint discoloration. You have to look carefully to be sure it's really there. It pays to remember that the fish are some way upstream of where this is seen. How far depends, of course, upon depth and current.

Bream don't seem to like bright light, and in summer they do most of their feeding at evening, through the night and in the early morning. But I have known plenty of exceptions, when big bream fed well right in the middle of the day, in shallow clear water — but this has always been in mild, showery weather, or when a good breeze has rippled the surface. The fish will feed in temperatures up to 68°F (20°C) and perhaps higher, and down to 40°F (4°C) but below 45°F (7°C) they feed much less freely than above, especially in still waters. In rivers, of course, there are plenty of times when the fish have been forced to swim against strong currents and under such conditions all fish feed at lower temperatures than would normally suit them.

In lakes, bream follow well-defined routes or 'beats' from which they seldom stray, even when tempted to do so by groundbait. It is important to study these routes, guided by discoloration of water, bubbles rising to the surface, fish rolling on the top, or information about catches. Bream send up small clusters of pea-sized bubbles that are easily identified.

As a final point, I read in Fred Taylor's book, *Angling in Earnest* that in the opinion of many successful bream fishers, the best time for big river bream is on mild nights in winter. What a change of view from that which was held for so many years, that bream were not worth trying to catch after October.

30

7 First you have to find your bream

The other day I had a letter from a young angler who wanted to know how to catch bream in a canal near his home and who had been told by local anglers that the bream there were uncatchable. In case any other readers are in a similar position, here is the letter I wrote in reply:

'There is no such thing as a bream that can't be caught, but some bream are harder to catch than others. The most important thing is to find where they are, and that means spending time at the waterside watching for signs of the bream shoals. These are most often seen either early in the morning or late in the evening and the three things to watch for are:
1 Bream rolling on the surface.
2 Mud stirred up by bream digging in the bottom.
3 Bubbles coming up where bream have disturbed the bottom mud.
The amount of mud stirred up depends on how many bream are in the shoal and how muddy the bottom is. You seldom see great clouds of mud; more often you need to look carefully to spot where the water is just a tiny bit muddier than elsewhere. Of course bream aren't feeding all the time, so you need to do quite a lot of walking about the banks to be sure of spotting the mud-stain when feeding starts. All too often, by the time it starts it is too dark to see it. So morning rather than evening gives you a better chance.

The bubbles bream send up are usually about pea-size and come to the surface in strings of from four to five up to twenty or more. Where there is a feeding shoal you can often see a whole lot of strings of unbroken bubbles on the surface, particularly if it is calm.

Once you have found the places where the bream feed, you can start groundbaiting, and I think the best and cheapest groundbait is stale bread — well soaked and mashed up to a soft pulp, then stirred up well with a dry groundbait — or plain sausage rusk, until it is just stiff enough to make into balls, each about the size of a small orange.

If you can put a dozen such balls in a bream feeding place every day for a week, at the time when you have found the bream usually feed, you should be able to catch quite a few when you start fishing. For bait, use bread paste, flake or crust. If this fails, you can try groundbaiting with small red worms enclosed in balls of mud, using the same worms as hook-bait. In some waters the bream prefer bread, in others worms, but bread is usually successful and involves less trouble than gathering enough worms for a week's ground-baiting.

The odd thing about bream is the way they suddenly start and stop feeding. It is quite possible to have your bait lying right in the middle of a shoal of bream without getting a bite, sometimes for hours, and then suddenly they start feeding and you catch one after another, until they stop just as suddenly as they started.

Although they usually feed best at dawn and dusk, they do start at other times, so if you bait-up a place, don't be in too much of a hurry to move if you don't catch fish straight away. I have often sat for as long as five or six hours before bream began to bite, but then had big catches.

You may take weeks to find the right spots and start catching the bream, so don't be disappointed if your first attempts fail. People think I am a good angler but I'm not really. The reason why I have caught a lot of good big fish is that I don't give up trying, once I have decided to go after some fish I know about, and this is the real secret of success. Any fish can be caught if an angler can find the right place, the right time, the right tackle, the right method and the right bait, and if he takes care not to scare the fish he is after. But you don't always get all these things right the first time you try. I don't anyway.

Don't make the mistake of fishing too fine or using hooks

that are too small, because if you get broken-up by the fish you hook, or if the hook comes away, you may not get any more bites. I would use 3lb or 4lb line and a No 12 or No 10 hook — nothing weaker or smaller.

Perhaps I should add that in some canals it may be very difficult to locate the bream by seeing them rolling, spotting mud-stains or observing bubbles, particularly where there is much boat traffic. There is another trick you can try in such cases, though it takes a lot of time and effort. The equipment you need consists of a small plastic basin, a tin can and some string.

You make three holes in the tin near its open end, and attach a string to each hole, joining them all together and tying them to a longer string that will reach nearly across the canal. Then you put a stone inside the tin, and chuck it out by swinging the string and then letting go. When you pull it in again, it will contain a sample of mud from the canal bottom and you can wash this in the plastic basin, like a prospector panning for gold, so as to see what creatures are in the mud, such as bloodworms, water snails, shrimps, pea mussels and other animals. In this way you can find out which stretches of the canal are richest in fish-food. Obviously the bream will prefer these stretches, and so will other bottom-feeding fish like carp and tench, if your canal also holds these species.

If I were you, I'd give bread — or worms — a thorough trial because I expect quite a lot of fishing is done on your canal, mostly by anglers using maggots, and if so, many of the fish, and probably nearly all the bigger fish will have learnt that maggots are unsafe to eat. I usually try bread first because it doesn't attract nuisance-fish like small perch or eels.

All the same, if your bait is among feeding bream you aren't likely to be bothered with perch, eels or indeed any other fish, even when using worm, because other species usually stay out of areas where bream are feeding.

Unless there is too much current in the canal, I would recommend you to use float tackle. And don't be afraid to use a fair-sized float and a fairly heavy shot, say a swan shot, because you want to anchor your bait where the groundbait is and not have it moved away by current or drift. You can attach the float by its bottom end only and sink the line. When bream are really feeding, they won't be put off by a biggish float and shot. I find it easier to wait for bites with float tackle because the float is there to watch, even if it doesn't move, and you don't get bored and start walking about, which may scare the fish.

One more thing, visit the canal in the close season, even though you can't fish. You may learn a few things that will help you to catch the bream when the season opens.'

8 How roach feed

Roach are very common and typically shoal fish. Much has been written about their natural food, but their wide distribution in waters of every kind makes it seem likely that there is little they will not eat, and that their diet varies considerably between one water and another.

There is no doubt, however, that they are more inclined to a vegetarian diet than other British fishes, and that they eat large quantities of algae, including a lot of green silkweed, when they can get it. They also eat various insects, worms, and water snails.

Their feeding methods resemble those of the bream to some extent, but they do not disturb the bottom as much, and they are more willing to take food brought down by the current, or, in still waters, food that is off the bottom. Like bream, they will sometimes feed right at the surface, but only rarely.

Preoccupation with one particular kind of food is commonly found in roach, and where heavy fishing is done, and large quantities of groundbait put in that consists of small food particles, it becomes very difficult to catch roach on any but very small baits. On waters that are not so treated, roach will take much bigger baits quite freely.

It is often said that fine tackle is needed to catch roach, but the truth is that the fine tackle is only needed when it is necessary to use very small baits, like maggots and hempseed. No fish is scared of nylon, however thick. But fish are suspicious of baits that behave differently from free particles of food. By groundbaiting with small particles of food, an angler forces himself to use very fine tackle. This is truer in roach fishing than in any other kind of angling, because the roach is the least tolerant of baits that are obviously tethered.

It is capable of taking in a bait and ejecting it like lightning if it feels any drag or check, and the shoal instinct among roach is so strong that if one roach rejects a bait, all the other fish in the shoal will usually refuse to touch it.

The effect of light on the feeding of roach is enormous, and while the smaller fish will feed at almost any time, and at all temperatures from 70°F (21°C) or more down to 40°F (4°C) and sometimes to near freezing point, the better fish do not like to feed in bright light. There is in fact a lot of evidence to show that there is a very definite point in the fading of light at which big roach commence to feed in earnest, and another, as the light increases, at which they stop. Of course, it is the light where the roach are that matters — down near the bottom — and obviously, if the water is deep and coloured, they will feed when the light at the surface is greater than they would tolerate in clear, shallow water. I am sure that where roach are concerned, light is a more important factor than water temperature. Even in water that is so lacking in oxygen that trout are seriously distressed, roach will come on feed heartily as the light fades. They keep feeding long after dark, too. How long seems to vary between one water and another, but with most fish, including roach, there is a dead spell around midnight when nothing much is done. Of course, they start feeding again before dawn, and carry on until the light gets too bright for them.

I must stress that all this applies to the larger roach. In fact, with every fish, the bigger they get, the fussier they become about the conditions of temperature, oxygen and light in which they will feed. Little fish of all kinds will feed under almost all conditions, as a rule.

Light not only affects when roach — and some other fish — will feed but also where they feed. At dusk, or when heavy colour in the water makes it dusk as far as the roach are concerned, the fish will move into very shallow water and feed there. An angler may at such times be fruitlessly fishing well out in the deeps, with big roach feeding under his rod.

I said earlier that roach were more inclined than bream to intercept baits coming down the current or to feed at mid-water, and this is true. But the bigger the roach, the less true it becomes. Big roach are often taken on moving baits, or baits off the bottom, because after all there are no rules without exceptions, and roach are common enough to make even the exceptions add up to sizeable numbers.

Added to that is the fact that for every angler fishing a stationary bait on the bottom, there are probably fifty either trotting down, or fishing a slow-sinking bait on a 'long trail', and it is no wonder that enough large roach are caught by such methods to obscure the truth.

This is, that if you want specimen roach, your best bet by far is a stationary bait fished on the bottom — in poor light. I have caught several hundred roach upwards of 2lb but I doubt if I've had a dozen on baits that were off the bottom or moving in any way.

I am fortunate in having been able to observe the behaviour of roach in three separate rivers where the water is clear enough to allow the fish to be seen easily, and in all these rivers the roach run to good size. When the light is bright, the big roach, in shoals of from ten to fifty or more, swim backwards and forwards, round and about, quite aimlessly. And they completely ignore any bait you may offer. You can catch little roach and dace in these swims at such times, on baits such as maggots or hemp, and if you couldn't see the big ones, you'd think none were there. But when the light begins to fail, these big chaps get their noses down. If you've put in some pieces of paste as groundbait, and can see them as white specks on the bottom, you notice them beginning to disappear one by one. This you can see long after it has become too dark to see the fish themselves.

Your off-bottom bait still catches only the babies, up to four ounces or so. So you slide the float up, put on a bigger bait, and lay-on. It is then that the good fish, from twelve ounces up to two-pounders, take firmly and are caught one after another.

Of course, we have to bear in mind the odd times when big roach feed in bright sunshine, for although they are rare, no one wants to miss the chance when it comes.

First of all, like barbel, big roach will sometimes take silkweed as hook-bait in bright sunshine and fast runs of water. Then there are times when they will take maggots, or caddis, in the narrow runs between the large areas of trailing weeds that grow on the broad shallows, especially in the early part of the season. And sometimes, big roach suddenly decide to eat freshwater shrimps — and they'll do it in very bright conditions, too. Why the roach do it once in a blue moon, when there are loads of shrimps about all the year round, I don't know. But it does happen, and if you're there and seize your chance, you may make a remarkable catch.

9 Roach fishing in winter

Veteran readers will remember the sport we had on the Upper Ouse back in the 1960s, using crayfish as bait. Lately, some friends and I have been having some fun with the roach there, with an occasional pike to liven things up. The fishing has been quite orthodox, but there are one or two small points it has brought to mind that may be helpful to some readers.

The first is that the bigger roach seem to like the swims that used to be 'cabbage patches' in summer. 'Cabbage patches' are the places where there are plenty of water-lily plants, but just too much current to let their leaves come to the top and lie flat in the ordinary manner. The leaves are therefore under water, and grow in a crinkly sort of way that looks somewhat like a lettuce or cabbage. So we call the places where they grow 'cabbage patches'. Lots of them are almost unfishable in the summer, though if you can find an opening there is no knowing what you may pull out of it — often a decent perch or a chub, as well as roach. In winter, however, these 'cabbage patches' die down and all that remains are a few odd bits of root on the bottom. Having seen the places in summer is a great help, as you can find a bit of bottom that is pretty free from roots.

Whether there is some organism that feeds on the last remnants of decaying leaves and on which the roach feed in turn, or whether the roach choose these spots in winter because they are usually deeper places anyway, I don't quite know, but it is beyond doubt that where there were 'cabbages' in summer, there the roach will be in winter — unless there is a heavy spate, considerably altering the set of the current.

We don't find trotting tactics much good in a 'cabbage patch' because you're always catching up on roots and dead stalks. The way to fish is to find a bit of open bottom — a couple of square yards is enough — and lay-on. If you aren't sure of the bottom it pays to search thoroughly with a plummet and find the exact spot, otherwise your bait may be caught under a root or leaf and catch nothing.

Much depends on the current, but we usually find one good big shot, and a quill float to suit it, about right. Crust and flake make good baits and if either is chosen the shot only needs to be two or three inches from the hook. The float is set about a foot or so further from the shot than the depth of the water, and after casting the rod is set in a rest and the line drawn in till the float cocks properly. If it lies a bit slantwise, it won't matter.

You have to keep your hand on the rod butt, because the fish will soon have the bait off if you don't hit them quickly, but although you must not waste time, you don't have to strike like super-greased-lightning. Remember the bite may be a flat-float one, if a fish lifts the shot.

I have used maggots a lot, but we seem to get a much better average size of roach on crust or flake. We've mostly used 12 and 14 hooks on 2lb bs line; but I tried a No 10 on 5lb bs line last time and caught just as many roach as the others using finer tackle. If you are only wanting roach, you'll do better to stick to the light line and a delicate rod, because you'll have more fun; but you mustn't mind getting smashed when the big chub comes along, as he almost certainly will if you sit quietly and low. If you want to land him, you can use the stouter gear and still catch plenty of good roach.

I think mashed-bread groundbait is as good as anything for getting fish on feed, which sometimes takes quite a time. Irrespective of when we do get the fish on feed, we seem to catch the most and biggest in the last hour of daylight, even when it has begun to freeze quite hard. We haven't caught any very big ones, though Fred Taylor lost one that looked all of 2½lb. The average catch has usually included one or two pounders, with an odd fish over the 1½lb mark for one of us.

I do not mean to suggest that this is the only way or even the best way to fish for roach in winter, but anglers who know of 'cabbage patches' in the rivers they fish may find it worth giving them a try with our way of fishing.

10 How dace feed

The dace is another typical shoal fish, and what I have already said about shoal behaviour applies fully to it. But there is a very important difference between the dace and the other species with which I have dealt so far. These other species don't like too much light, but will feed freely when the light has faded. Dace are diametrically opposite in their preference. They will feed freely in bright sunshine, but once the light has fallen below a certain level, they stop feeding.

In all my experience the pattern of feeding of roach and dace has been complementary, in that the dace are going off just at the time the roach are coming on, as the dusk of evening begins to fall. Now, of course, everyone knows that roach and dace are taken by anglers more or less together, from the same swim, especially small ones of both species. But when it comes to the good-sized fish, dace upwards of about ½ lb and roach around the 1lb mark, the difference in feeding behaviour, according to the light, is very noticeable.

The main food of dace is insects of all kinds, and they also eat quite a lot of crustaceans including fresh-water shrimps. They obtain a big proportion of their food by taking up a favourable position — as a shoal — to intercept what comes down with the current, provided the current is sufficient, which it usually is in waters inhabited by dace. It is worth remembering, however, that when a river is dead low and the current is slight, or in cases where dace have been put into still waters, the dace shoals will rove about looking for food. In drought conditions on many rivers I fish, dace shoals quarter wide areas of shallow water and fishing for them demands keen observation and long, accurate casting.

On those rivers that have big surface hatches of fly, dace do a tremendous amount of surface feeding, and, of course, during the process they intercept numerous nymphs that are rising to the surface. Dace can become every bit as preoccupied with one sort of fly as can trout, and when fishing for them with artificial fly, it is often found necessary to offer them a reasonable imitation of the fly on the water. On rivers of that kind, I am sure that fly fishing, in summer and autumn, is the very best way to catch specimen dace.

In Hertford museum there is a case of eight dace all over 1lb, taken by the same angler on fly from the River Beane, and H. T. Sheringham took four dace over 1lb in a single season from the Kennet, all, I believe, on fly. I myself had three, 1lb 1oz, 1lb 2oz and 1lb 5oz, in three successive casts from the River Cam.

When dace are in shallow water, or feeding near or at the surface, but are not interested solely in one species of insect, I use a special fly that I have found absolutely deadly, provided it is presented correctly. It is tied on a No 16 hook and has a body made of greenish peacock herl, a rather sparse, longish hackle from a black cock, and a bunch of blue dun hackle-fibres, tied slanting backwards, for a wing. That is for fishing it floating. For fishing sunk, the cock hackle is replaced by a feather from the breast of a cock starling, wound as a hackle, but only about three turns. The tying silk is dark brown.

One insect that big dace often become very interested in is the daddy longlegs. When these are getting onto the water in large numbers, the dace go quite mad about them and won't look at anything else. You can dap these chaps or if the situation prevents dapping, you can try using a bubble float or an ordinary float with lead wire wrapped round the middle and no shot. Live bluebottle can be used in the same way. Alternatively, the nearly forgotten art of blow-line fishing can be applied.

I have mentioned these methods because the dace is mainly an insect-eating fish, but it does eat other things, especially in rivers where insect life is somewhat sparse. The fresh-water shrimp is eaten quite extensively and has the merit of being a thing that can be used as bait in its natural state, when dace are seen or suspected to be eating shrimps.

In conditions where there is no indication that the dace are being 'choosy', however, there is little advantage in collecting and using natural baits, because it is quite easy to catch the fish by either fly fishing, if the dace are at or near the surface, or by light-float fishing, with maggots as bait and groundbait, if the fish are lying deeper.

Where they are depends, I believe, more upon water temperature than anything else. You do not find them near the surface in very cold conditions. Dace don't mind cold weather so much as most other fish, but even so, they don't feed nearly so actively below 40°F (4°C) as they do above that temperature, and from about 48°F (9°C) downwards, they seem less willing to dart about. Instead they take up bottom-picking habits and from the angling point of view behave in much the same way as roach — except in their reaction to light conditions.

Now and then we find dace eating either little snails or silkweed. The little snails are picked off weeds and sometimes from submerged water-lily leaves. Fish eating them can usually be caught on hempseed, or, by putting in enough maggots, weaned off the snails. Dace eating silkweed or other algae such as that found growing on stones, wooden piles, etc, are more difficult to tempt. They are far less easy than some other kinds of fish to catch on silkweed used as hook-bait, and are not very easily persuaded to change their diet by offerings of maggots, seed or bread.

One well-known habit of dace — which they share with roach — remains to be mentioned. They eat elderberries, and when an elderberry bush is shedding its fruit into a suitable swim, anglers need no advice from me as to what bait to choose. Much the same applies to small green caterpillars falling into the water from bankside foliage.

11 Fish where it's weedy

I often fish a small river, one that is so clear that you can see every stone on the bottom, even in the deepest place. Where you can see the bottom at all, that is, because most of the river is a solid mass of bright-green, waving weeds.

At first sight, you'd think it was both fishless and unfishable. Many anglers pass over it on the way to a bigger and less-weedy river, although neither ticket nor rod licence is needed to fish it. But walk carefully along it, and presently you will see that there are narrow, gravel-bottomed runs here and there among all those weeds. And if you keep perfectly still, you will see a fish swing out from under the weeds, across the run and under the weeds on the other side. It will be followed by another and another, until perhaps a dozen have crossed. After a while, they all cross back, one or two stopping momentarily to pick up something from the bottom.

They are dace, and it takes you a little time to realise what big ones they are — why, half that shoal must be pounders, you think! Walk on, if you like, looking for a shoal in a place you can easily fish. You won't find one, though, so you may as well resign yourself to solving the problem that fishing these runs between the weeds presents.

One way is to fish with roach pole, float tackle, and hemp. It is possible to succeed that way; I've done it myself, but it is an arm-breaking business. You see, you'll be lucky if your float can travel four feet without fouling weed, and the surface current is very quick. So it's in, out, in, out, at four-second intervals, and while you will perhaps get an odd fish before your arm cries enough, it isn't really a very satisfactory method.

What I like to do is choose a run where I can see the bottom very clearly, preferably from behind some cover like tall grass, bushes, or willow herb. I put on a single large shot, about three inches from a No 14 hook on a 2lb monofil line. If I can, I pick a run where I can lower the bait straight down; that makes things much easier. The rod goes in a rest.

Well, you can use maggots if you like, or little red worms, but if you do not mind doing a bit of paddling, I'd recommend caddis grubs. No, don't put any water in the tin; they live longer if they are kept just moist. Put one on the hook. You have lowered it to the bottom; well, it will serve to teach you what happens if you do. How many minnows flew at it and whipped it off your hook? No! not really ten thousand! Only about two hundred, I'd say.

Put on another one, but this time don't present it to those minnows. Just let it hang, touching the surface, and wait till you see the dace begin to cross the swim. You may have to wait a few minutes, but not, as a rule, so long as to try your patience unduly.

Here they come; now let it drop all of a sudden. One, two, three, four, taking no notice . . . but this one has seen it, he is going for it — no, turned away, and now they've all gone again. Leave it as long as the minnows will . . . No, you will have to pull it up and re-bait.

No, you can't expect a bite every time the dace appear; but stick at it. One will make a mistake presently. Here they come again; the second one's going right for it, he's got it, strike!

Twelve ounces, a very nice dace; but now you will have to wait quite a while for another from that run. I think you'd do best to try another place.

You can go on like this, getting a fish here and there, feeding three out of four of your baits to the minnows, missing more dace than you hook, and nearly always rolling over one that looks near record size; sweating, sometimes swearing, getting stung by nettles and bitten by flies, all through a hot summer day. You may catch as many as ten dace; once I got six, one of which was a pounder.

It is worth all the trouble, when you could come in the winter, with the weed down and the water coloured, and trot a maggot down to catch thirty or forty fish? (At least, I suppose you could; I have never tried. It wouldn't seem quite fair, to me.)

I think it is well worth it; if you get fish, you really feel you've accomplished something. But more important still, you will learn more about the behaviour and habits of dace in one day spent scratching in the runs between the weeds than you could in years fishing where your only indication of a bite is the movement of your float.

12 How rudd feed

You've only got to look at a rudd to see that it is well equipped for taking food it sees above it, for it has a decidedly upturned mouth. Because of this mouth, the rudd is usually called a surface feeder, but although rudd do feed at the surface quite often, they also feed near the bottom and at all depths in between.

Scientists say that insects form the main part of the rudd's diet, but scientists have a habit of examining the stomach contents of small, easily caught fish and assuming that bigger ones of the same species eat the same food, which, unfortunately for their calculations, is by no means always true. It is not in the case of rudd, for big rudd eat lots of water snails, and, when they get the chance, numbers of small fish, as well as insects. I have no doubt that they also eat any fresh-water mussels that are small enough to swallow, for big rudd, like big tench, always seem to be found in waters that are clear and hold lots of swan mussels.

A big rudd is ideally built for coming up and picking snails, and snail spawn, off the under side of water-lily leaves, and you don't need to spend long beside a pool holding rudd before you see the fish doing it. As for eating fish, a really small fish, or a tiny spinner, is one of the very best baits for a big rudd, and when fly fishing, a 'fly' that imitates a little fish always does well if fished correctly. In fact, it is sometimes possible to catch rudd on a bare, bright-gilt crystal hook, with nothing whatever in the way of bait on it at all.

In reed-fringed lakes, rudd spend most of the daylight hours in the reed-beds where, no doubt, they find plenty of food such as insects and water snails, and where they are sheltered from the attacks of pike and other predators. They move into open water when the light begins to fail.

So much for what rudd eat. When will they feed? Well, it would be hard to find a fish more willing to feed at any time of day or night, in any condition of light, than the rudd. But they do seem to be keener to feed at dusk and at dawn, during the summer at any rate. I have never known water temperature to rise so high that rudd refused to feed, and in still-water fishing they often provide sport in heat-wave conditions that have put every other species well off. At the opposite extreme, rudd can sometimes still be caught, for they will feed close to the bottom when the temperature at the surface is near freezing point.

One difficulty is to find where they are. But that is nothing compared to the difficulty of finding and catching rudd when the water is too cold for them to feed near the surface or on the shallows, but not cold enough to drive them into the extreme depths. In these intermediate conditions, shoals of rudd rove about at midwater or thereabouts, and when you have to find the correct feeding depth *and* the right spot, and the shoals aren't even in any one spot for long, catching them is far more a matter of luck than of angling knowledge and skill. In fact, all angling knowledge can tell you is why you can't catch 'em!

Unlike many other species of fish, rudd seldom become pre-occupied with eating one particular kind of food, and if you can locate them, you can usually tempt them with any of the common baits, like bread, maggots or worms. A good rudd will take the very biggest lobworm you can find and where there are lots of little rudd, a big worm helps you to pick out the bigger fish. So does a big floating crust, either cast out or fished margin-wise, under the rod top, at dusk or after dark in warm weather.

I've just been talking to an angler who regularly catches more and bigger rudd than most fishermen, and he tells me that he does very well with cockles as hook-bait. He gets them from the fishmonger and soaks them overnight to get most of the salt out. He warns me that there are few worse smells than a bait box full of cockles left over from last week! I expect the rudd take the cockles for snails that have somehow lost their shells. Anyhow, they like 'em, and so do big bream.

If you like fly fishing for rudd and want to catch specimen fish, remember that a big rudd dearly loves a Great Red Sedge fly, *Phryganea grandis* or *Phryganea striata*, whichever happens to live in your lake. In case you've never seen one, it's a whopping great moth-like insect which buzzes, zooms and struggles about on the surface. And you can tie a fine imitation of it on a long-shanked No 8 hook, in exactly the same shape as the white-moth imitation.

Only, for the big sedge, you use ginger hackles, and a bit of speckly partridge-wing-feather fibre for the wing. You move it in little jerks on the surface after you've made your cast. Of course, the white moth itself does pretty well, too.

There are times when rudd will pick baits off the very bottom, but I do believe that when rudd are near bottom you catch them better with a bait several inches off it, either hanging below a float or, in the case of crust, floating about four or five inches up above a lead on the bottom. It saves the rudd the trouble of standing on their heads.

13 Reed-bed rudd pack a punch

I suppose that the rudd is one of our most neglected fish. It isn't exactly rare, yet how often do you hear an angler say that he had been rudd fishing, or that he is even interested in it?

It is hard to understand this, because the rudd is an exceptionally beautiful fish, which grows bigger than the roach and in my experience, weight for weight, fights harder. Of course, there aren't so many ways of fishing for rudd as there are for roach, nor do you find rudd in such a wide range of different waters as those that hold roach. Roach are more interesting, in that they are usually craftier and harder to catch, whereas rudd can sometimes be very easy indeed. I suppose that is why so many anglers, like me, prefer roach fishing, but fortunately we do not have to choose one or the other. We can fish for both.

The kind of rudd fishing I like best is where I can sit in a boat or better still, a nice, stable punt anchored just the right distance from an extensive reed-bed. There are two ways of fishing from a craft so anchored: float fishing and fly fishing.

Whichever method you use, the essential thing is to put the bait or the fly right up against the reed stems, even right in among them if you can see one or two places where the reeds aren't too closely spaced, or little gaps or bays in the forest of reeds. This is especially true in the middle part of the day. In the early morning and late evening, the rudd venture farther out into the open water, but when the light is bright they stay right in those reeds.

You may ask, why risk hang-ups and tackle losses by fishing close to or actually among the reeds, when by waiting till evening or fishing early, you could avoid the necessity?

I look on rudd as what might be called 'fill-in' fish. In the early morning and late evening, I'm usually after tench, or bream, or carp, and I fill in the middle hours of the day by going after the rudd. That's only one reason, though. Another is that I find it more fun to catch rudd that take extra skill to catch. To catch them when they are in the reeds demands much more skill; the casting has to be dead accurate for distance, and if you are aiming for a small gap, it needs to be accurate for direction as well.

In float fishing, I like to use a green, tapered balsa float attached by a rubber tube at each end, so that it will go through the reeds either way without catching their stems. The best leads to use are those long thin French ones, like elongated split shot.

If the bottom is fairly hard, I find that a good-sized worm on a No 10 hook is an excellent bait and I have a notion that in such conditions worm attracts a higher average size of rudd than bread baits. Large grubs and caterpillars are also very good. On a soft bottom, however, I think crust cubes are preferable, fished with the lead only a few inches from the hook, which will produce 'lift', or flat-float, bite-indications.

It does not pay to use ultra-fine tackle for this sort of fishing because if you are lucky you may hook a 2lb or even a 3lb fish only inches from dense reeds — sometimes actually in among the reeds — and then you simply must hold the fish hard to prevent it charging right in. I usually fish 4 or 5lb line, and I do not think I get any fewer bites than I would with finer stuff.

Within reason, I do not think that it matters much what sort of rod and reel you use for this kind of fishing. Nowadays I usually choose a lightweight 12ft carbon one, with a small high-geared reel, although I have also used a 9ft carbon rod, made to a fly-rod design but with an 18in parallel cork handle and sliding rod fittings, mainly because it is very accurate.

For real accuracy, you cannot beat fly-fishing tackle. Catching rudd with this is great fun. With the boat or punt anchored about twenty yards from the edge of the reeds, you can drop a fly accurately in every little gap, let it sink and then draw slowly and steadily. It seldom pays to draw more than a yard or so before lifting off and casting again.

Rudd aren't very fussy about fly they will take, but my favourite is a green nymph with its rear-half ribbed with narrow gold tinsel. I put a couple of layers of fine copper wire, close-wound, on the hook shank before anything else, so as to make the nymph sink positively and fairly quickly.

Water near reeds is usually shallow but sometimes there are quite deep places and it is a great help to have been along a day or so before fishing and checked the depths. With the float tackle you get a more or less automatic check, but not with the fly rod and nymph. It is important to let the nymph sink well down in the deeper places.

Don't run away with the idea that only green nymphs will catch rudd. They will take almost any wet fly, properly fished, but they seem particularly keen on those with gold tinsel in the dressing, like Dunkeld, Cinnamon and Gold Butcher, and so on.

On one lake I used to fish, you could catch them with a bare gilt hook, and even better if the gilt hook had a few turns of peacock herl just behind the eye. Much more important than the fly pattern is putting the fly right up against or among the reeds, where the fish are. Like perch, they don't care to come far out of the reed jungle when the light is bright.

Talking about perch, there is a fair chance of catching these instead of rudd when you are working the reed fringes with a worm on float tackle or with a fly. (In the latter case it is best to use a different sort of fly if it *is* perch you want — something like a Polystickle, a big Alexandra, a Sweeny Todd or a Hanningfield Lure.)

With the green nymph, you may find yourself attached to something a good deal more powerful than either rudd or perch, in the shape of a tench. Of course that can also happen with the float tackle and worm or breadcrust bait.

After you have caught some rudd in a spot, you'll generally find they seem to stop feeding. Mark the spot where you caught them, move off and fish somewhere else for an hour or so, then come back and fish that spot again and you will generally get a few more.

It isn't easy to do this sort of fishing from the bank, but even then, remember rudd are right in the reeds. If you have a gap through which you can fish, don't do as so many anglers do and cast a long way out. Fish close to the outer edges of the reeds, to one side or the other of your gap. You will almost always find that one side is far more productive than the other, so try both till you discover which side is best.

Rudd fishing can be fine sport, if you go about it in the right way.

14 How tench feed

The tench is not very easy to classify as a shoal fish or otherwise. Although tench undoubtedly do move in shoals at times, there are always numbers of individual fish by themselves, in any water that holds numbers of tench. And when tench are gathered together in a shoal, they do not follow one another's example in the same way as do roach, bream or dace.

Because your bait is refused by one tench, it does not mean that it is sure to be refused by others in the vicinity, and you are not likely to find that losing a fish means that the shoal is scattered.

If plenty of feeding tench are in your pitch, the chances are that you'll keep on catching them, and it is quite possible you may also catch the one you lost earlier.

Not enough is known about what tench live on, but it is certain that they eat lots of the bloodworms that live in the bottom mud, and that they dig quite deeply into that mud to get them. When they are feeding keenly on these bloodworms, in a soft-mud bottom, they are quite difficult to catch. They also eat quantities of water snails, which they pick off the bottom and off growing weed. No doubt they eat plenty of water insects of all kinds, especially the slower-moving kinds, like caddis. They are very fond of fresh-water mussel, and while I doubt if there is any way in which they can eat the big ones, I expect they eat plenty of baby mussels.

When they are feeding at the bottom, tench send up bubbles which are characteristic of this species, being quite small, little bigger than a pin's head. The quantity of bubbles depends on how much gas is trapped in the bottom. Few bubbles come up from a sand or gravel bottom; great quantities from deep soft mud. Where modest quantities of bubbles are seen rising, a bait cast among them is very likely to be taken, but over soft bottoms from which large volumes of bubbles come up, getting a bite from a tench is very difficult, as I have explained.

For some reason, feeding tench do not stir up mud and colour the water to any great extent, unlike carp and bream, but they often betray their whereabouts by rolling at the surface, which I think is usually a preliminary to feeding.

Tench are greatly influenced both by light and by water temperature. Below 60°F (16°C) the chances of catching tench decrease steadily as the temperature falls, until at 50°F (10°C) or less the fish are simply not eating.

Of course, exceptions are found at times, usually when flood-water has made the fish use energy which they need to replace by feeding. Above 70°F (21°C) the fish again become unwilling to feed, and by knowing whereabouts in a lake the temperature will best suit the fish, one can often catch tench at times when other anglers are beaten.

There is plenty of reason to think that tench dislike too-bright light, though they are less exacting in their reactions to light than are big roach. They tend to move, however, into deeper swims as the light gets brighter in the morning, and then into the shallows again as it fails in the evening. Since, however, the light gets brighter as the air gets warmer on most summer days, and vice versa, it is often difficult to know whether it is the light or the temperature which has most effect upon the fish.

On warm summer nights, tench often come right in close to the bank, feeding upon anything they can find on the bottom or the marginal vegetation, and I fancy this habit originated from a search for such things as snails, both the land and water varieties, and slugs, etc, that are found at the margins. These margin-feeding tench will, however, take almost anything edible they come across, including paste on the bottom or floating crusts.

The angler who stays on for an hour or two after dark at a tench water may often get a fish, which is seldom a small one, by fishing within a couple of feet of the bank, when fishing well out would have been fruitless. For some curious reason, tench will sometimes come right in to the bank, and feed among the reeds and rushes in the shallows on really sweltering hot, sunny days, which would appear to contradict what has been said about their not liking too much light.

Of course, we find similar exceptional behaviour among other species of fish, but the wise angler fishes according to the usual behaviour of the fish he is after, with one eye cocked for unusual happenings. The tench feeding in marginal stems in bright sunshine is a very different customer from the tench feeding in the margins at night. The daytime ones are hard to tempt and the best bet is a small bait, like a snail, a maggot, or a grain of wheat or hemp, fished off the bottom and on tackle that lets it sink slowly. Tench are not fast biters, but the smaller the bait, the sooner they spit it out when they feel the line, so when fishing with small baits it is necessary to strike quite quickly.

When picking baits off the bottom, or digging into the mud, tench stand on their heads with their tails pointing almost straight up, and for that reason tackle should be arranged in such a manner that the line doesn't run straight up above the bait, otherwise a fish may find it quite difficult to get the bait into its mouth.

I have described this effect fully in my book *Still-Water Angling*, and many people have since asked how, if this is what happens, the 'lift' method can work. Well, it isn't suggested that it is not possible to catch tench with the line running straight up and down, only that it reduces your chances to fish so.

The lift method, properly fished, doesn't have the line running vertically, anyway. The float is set at a distance from the shot about 30 per cent greater than the depth of the water, so that the line from shot to float is at a good angle. Even then, it is not ideal for tench that are feeding really heartily. It is a method for tricky tench, that need striking quickly before they can spit out the bait.

For tench that mean to *eat* your bait, it is best to have upwards of twelve inches, or more, between shot and baited hook — to give the tench a good chance of picking up the bait without running foul of the line.

A lot remains to be learned about the behaviour and feeding of tench, and I certainly don't profess to know it all. What exercises the minds of many is the problem of the very big tench. I have said before that there are many waters in which exist tench well over the present record, up to twelve pounds or so. They can be seen at times, yet these fish are never caught. Do they live on foods quite different from what smaller tench eat? Do they feed in different conditions? Or are their numbers so small that the mathematical odds against one taking an angler's bait are altogether too great?

15 Find cold water and you'll find those big tench

This season I've done more tench fishing than usual. I've done it in various places and by various methods, and some things that have happened have puzzled me. Others have fitted into the fabric of what I already knew.

Tench move about a lot and I am increasingly convinced that the commonest reason for not catching them is that we spend hours fishing in the wrong place at the wrong time. However, it is true that sometimes they aren't feeding at all, and at others they're feeding on bloodworms, or some other natural food.

Tench do not like water that is too warm, and they shift about accordingly. During a recent hot spell, the only place I could catch tench was at the bottom of the deepest place I could find. The water temperature at the surface, all over the lake, was above 70°F (21°C). In the interests of angling science (and not because I was so hot that I was in danger of being reduced to a grease-spot), I dived to the bottom of that deep hole, about eleven or twelve feet. The bottom three feet or so of water was so cold that I should have gasped if I'd been able to! Later in the day the tench went off, even in the deep hole.

As the sun went down and the sky turned red, unmistakable tench bubbling commenced on the shallows — which were naturally cooling faster than the deeps. I fished for these bubbling tench, missed one and hooked and lost another; water temperature had gone down to 65°F (18°C). Around midnight I made another move, to water not deeper than ten or twelve inches. Legering with lob, I had a bite first throw, and missed it. About 2am I had another bite and caught a tench, 4lb 2oz; water temperature, 63°F (17°C).

After daybreak, when the mist stopped rising off the water, showing that its temperature had begun to rise, all signs of tench on those shallows ceased. All this confirms my opinion that in hot weather, tench move to where it is coolest, and in a lake that is generally shallow they move into very shallow places in the late evening and after dark. If there are deep holes — deep enought to retain some cool water at the bottom — the tench will go there in the heat of the day. If not, they'll stop feeding, and if it gets very hot they'll come to the surface and lie about under weeds or lily pads.

You can catch big tench after dark, in many waters, by fishing right in the margin, only inches from the bank. I have caught several on floating crust while margin fishing for carp, during hot spells of weather.

Quite recently, Maurice Ingham, Pete Thomas and the Taylor brothers all went tench fishing together. They fished from an island. Ken and Joe Taylor fished the deeper water, ten to twelve feet. Fred, Maurice and Pete fished in depths of four or five feet. They had a number of tench over 4lb and up to 5½lb. Ken and Joe had some nice rudd from the deeps, but never touched a tench. All the fish were caught between 7am and 10am. The weather was rainy and rather chilly, with water temperature between 60°F (16°C) and 62°F (17°C). I think if the day had turned out hot, Ken and Joe would have started catching tench after the others had stopped.

We still have much to learn about tench. Why, for example, they roll about the surface like pigs in one water, and never show in another. Why, in waters where you can see whacking great tench, double-figure ones, not just odd fish, but several that size, you can fish and fish and never catch anything over about 5 to 5½lb. Do these monster tench have feeding habits radically different to those of their smaller brethren? Or are thay just much craftier?

I know and fish three waters where tench of ten, eleven and even twelve pounds exist without a shadow of doubt, yet I cannot even claim to have hooked one, let alone caught one of that size in any of these lakes. Perhaps one day the puzzle will be solved.

16 How carp feed

A great deal has been written about carp in recent years, but by no means everything is known about their feeding habits. It seems likely that in most waters these fish live mainly upon chironomid larvae; that is, the larvae of various species of midge flies. There are many of these larvae in the mud. A well-known kind is the bloodworm, which may also be found in water butts.

No doubt carp also eat all kinds of insects, water snails, mussels, and some kinds of plants, including algae, but the only things besides chironomid larvae that may form a significant part of their diet are small crustacea, of which daphnia and cyclops are common kinds. The fact that duckweed vanishes when carp are introduced into a water in numbers means little, because duckweed is not found in waters where carp are established. They may clear it up when first introduced, but they don't live on it.

With the exception of mussels and water snails — and we have no evidence that these are eaten in any quantity — the whole diet of carp consists of very small things, too small by far to use as hook-bait, at any rate on a hook big enough to land a big carp. Even if it were possible, it would not be very successful, because the carp are not eating bloodworms, or daphnia, one at a time.

What happens is that the carp uses its mouth like a vacuum cleaner, sucking in mouthfuls of daphnia, or of mud full of larvae. In the latter case, I think the mouthful is swallowed, mud, larvae and all. Carp dig quite deeply into the bottom mud to obtain their food. The fact that the natural food of carp consists of those small things, and that when feeding on them the fish simply fail to recognise anything else as food, is one of the main difficulties with which the carp fisher has to contend.

Another is the sensitivity of carp to water temperature. I have never known them feed in water above 70°F (21°C), and every degree the temperature falls below 60°F (16°C) makes the chances of bites a great deal poorer. I would say the best temperature for carp to feed is between 62 and 65°F (17 and 18°C), but of course there are many instances of carp feeding well below this range. During summer, the temperature of the water frequently changes from above to below this range, and back again, and this means that, quite often, temperature puts carp off feed, and back on feed again. It may happen every day for weeks. This gives the carp fisher a chance to present his groundbait and hook-bait in such a way that the fish, coming on feed and moving towards natural feeding grounds, find the baited pitch first. This needs careful study to bring into effect, but it undoubtedly offers the best chance of catching carp, in the majority of waters.

Light affects the behaviour of carp considerably, but not, in my experience, their desire to feed or otherwise. I have observed them feeding heartily, and indeed have caught them, in all conditions of light from pitch-darkness to blazing midday sunshine. But on heavily fished waters, they generally keep well out from the banks until after dark. Whether this is because after dark they feel safer, or whether it is because at that time the fish-scaring type of angler has gone home, I cannot be sure. In waters of this type the fish often get into the habit of moving in close to the bank at dusk, in search of any tit-bits that may be there, like discarded sandwiches, groundbait, and the like. This habit, knowledge of which has brought me a lot of double-figure carp, may be dealt with by the method well-known nowadays as 'margin fishing'. It is not really a natural habit, and in dealing with other species I have not referred to it, but perhaps I should say here that not only carp, but tench, roach, rudd and chub also feed the same way in waters of the same kind, and may also be taken by margin-fishing methods.

With other species of fish I have mentioned how the way they pick up their food acts upon the angler's tackle in the form of bite-indications. With carp, the indication is usually quite unmistakable — lots of line goes out!

Some textbooks refer to carp nibbling and sucking at the bait. Undoubtedly they do this at times, but it is quite rare. I fancy most of the alleged nibblings of carp are really caused by fish too small to get the bait into their mouths.

Much more usual is the bite produced by a fish that has taken the bait well into its mouth and is running purposely away with it. There are times, however, when the indication is a very fast, short run, of perhaps two or three yards, perhaps more. Nearly every fish is missed on the strike, and when one is hooked, it is usually outside the mouth, often in a pectoral or ventral fin. On such occasions, bites come much more frequently than usual, and continually missing is most exasperating, especially when the fish are manifestly monstrous. There is nothing one can do about it, because the bait is being picked up delicately and carefully by the lips of the fish. The hook isn't in its mouth and you simply cannot hit the fish properly. The way in which carp can do this is quite uncanny.

Every summer I get numbers of letters from readers who have had these successions of terrific bites and missed the lot, and want to know what to do about it. I repeat, nothing can be done. If you wait instead of striking, the fish will not take the bait into its mouth eventually. It'll drop it. Not because it has become alarmed. It never meant to eat it, anyway. Why it picked it up in the first place, only the carp knows. I don't!

In the late 1940s and early 1950s, when much progress was made in discovering suitable tackle and methods for catching large carp, the baits used were big ones, chosen mainly to prevent their being taken by unwanted small fish. More recently, what have come to be known as 'particle' baits have proved effective. These consist of such things as sweet corn, stewed wheat, soaked dried peas, lentils and other seeds. Carp can be persuaded to eat such baits by regular generous pre-baiting, but then bite-indication poses problems. A carp feeding on sweet corn for example, in a baited-up area, does not swim away with each grain of corn it picks up, as it would with a boiled potato or ball of paste, the size of a pheasant's egg. It remains in the same spot, picking up grain after grain, often several at a mouthful, and swallowing them. The bite-indication usually takes the form of small pulls and twitches, and where possible a float should be used to detect these. For fishing after dark, one with a bright betalight top can be used.

Whenever it is suspected that the bait has been taken, it is probably wise to tighten gently, and if resistance is felt, to change from slow, gentle tightening to a fast, firm movement of the rod. If there is too much delay, the bait will have reached the throat teeth of the fish and the line will be bitten through.

Another recent development in carp baits involves the use of high-protein materials or additives. In my opinion, while in certain circumstances such baits are undoubtedly effective, rather too much confidence is placed in them. The fact is that where carp have not learnt, by being caught and released or hooked and lost, that certain foods are dangerous, they will eat almost anything, from low-protein foods like bread or potatoes, to high-protein substances like meat, cat food, dog food, liver or chicken guts. I once knew a keeper who used to paunch rabbits on the bank of a lake where no fishing was ever permitted, and throw the guts in the water, whereupon numerous large carp would eat them up in seconds. And we all know ornamental waters holding carp, where again no fishing is allowed, but where carp will take bread freely, even, sometimes, from one's fingers. Within a few weeks of taking up residence in the London Zoo aquarium, my 44lb record carp had learned to take food from the keeper's fingers — or mine — and was equally willing to eat low-protein bread or high-protein raw liver.

Advocates of high-protein paste baits invariably recommend an extensive and generous course of pre-baiting with these concoctions, and provided fishing with them does not commence prematurely, the results are usually very satisfactory. One must add that in many cases their ingredients include, as well as protein, flavours that carp find attractive.

One of the easiest to obtain and cheapest of high-protein baits are trout pellets. Choose the sinking kind for pre-baiting; soak some, pound them up and mix with brown breadcrumb to make a paste for hook-bait.

Like tench and bream, carp will often, when feeding, send up large quantities of bubbles but they differ from those sent up by tench and bream, in that they consist of bubbles of all sizes, from pinhead size to some nearly as big as a table-tennis ball. The quantity, of course, depends on how much natural gas there is in the water. Carp will also, at times, stir up the bottom mud enough to cause a great deal of discoloration of the water.

17 First, brainwash your carp

There has been some discussion in various quarters lately about the value of groundbaiting, especially for carp fishing.

Some very capable and successful carp anglers are saying that groundbaiting a swim before fishing has no advantage, and that it does not educate the fish into accepting the angler's hook-bait.

'Why,' it is asked, 'should a carp have to see quantities of a food before it begins to feed on it? If a carp sees, for example, twenty boiled potatoes on the bottom, it still has to take one of them first, which it is equally likely to do whether there is only one or twenty.'

Well, of course there are plenty of instances of carp and other fish taking single baits — even baits that have not previously been used on the water concerned — without any previous groundbaiting. Nobody suggests that unless pre-baiting is carried out, carp and other fish cannot be caught at all. But consider this. If fishing in a carp lake were to be altogether prohibited, and if someone went down to that lake every day with a bucketful of mashed bread, or boiled potatoes, and tipped them in, it would not be many weeks before he found large numbers of carp awaiting his arrival. And, when the food went in, they would feed freely on it without suspicion. Indeed there are ornamental lakes and pools here and there where this actually happens. In such waters, you wouldn't have many seconds to wait for a bite if you dropped a baited hook among the milling mass of fish.

Obviously, the more natural food there is in a lake, the longer it would take to make the fish accustomed to artificial feeding of that kind. The more fishing there is going on, the harder it becomes to get fish tame. But, generally speaking, I am well convinced that pre-baiting a swim or pitch does increase the angler's chances, not only by attracting fish to feed in a particular place but also by making them more willing to accept unnatural foods.

Consider the barbel in the Hampshire Avon. These fish are present in numbers from the mouth of the river up to Downton and above. Yet more than 99 per cent of those caught come from the Royalty fishery where, despite the extremely heavy fishing pressure, vast quantities of food are put in daily.

Since the use of maggot droppers became popular, there have been plenty of instances of barbel actually grabbing these droppers before they opened and released their contents. Those barbel are thoroughly brainwashed into taking maggots, simply because so many are constantly being put into the water. Believe me, it doesn't happen on other parts of the Avon! I have seen shoals of up to a dozen big barbel, absolutely refusing every bait that was offered them in the middle Avon. With a single exception — a fish that took worms, a much more natural bait — all the barbel I have ever taken in the middle Avon have been persuaded to take bunches of maggots, by feeding maggots steadily into the swims they inhabited, for hour after hour.

The fact is that fish are often in a state where they will not move to take a single item of food. It is not a question of their not being willing to move for a small food particle, but rather that it takes a succession of impacts upon their senses to awaken them to the fact that favourable feeding conditions are present. After such a succession of impacts — such as the repeated appearance of something eatable — fish may often start feeding. And when they do, they very frequently feed only on the kind of food that has aroused their interest. It is rather like programming a computer.

We see many instances of this in all kinds of fishing. Where hempseed is thrown into a roach water in considerable quantities, it often has the effect of making the roach difficult to catch on any other bait. When trout are feeding avidly on a hatch of some particular species of insect, they tend to ignore other insects, or other kinds of food, that may also be present in much smaller numbers.

If, as I do, you read as many angling books as you can lay your hands on, you will find numerous accounts of cases where fish knew exactly what they wanted and would not take anything else. One example that keeps cropping up is the falling of small green caterpillars into the water from overhanging trees. Fish congregating below to eat the caterpillars refuse normal flies and baits, but prove catchable when someone tries an artificial fly tied to imitate the caterpillars, or uses a green-dyed maggot, or one of the caterpillars themselves.

I could go on giving dozens of instances that support the general proposition that fish are often oblivious to single items of food but willing to feed on that food when larger quantities are available, often to the partial and sometimes total exclusion of other kinds of food. This can last for as long as the influence of the plentiful food persists.

This doesn't mean that all you have to do to catch fish is throw in huge quantities of groundbait day after day. You are still faced with the problem of how much you can put in without over-feeding the fish, and in some cases there is the problem of unwanted species being attracted.

Generally speaking, the problem is greatest with outsize fish. There must obviously be plenty of natural feed in the water in which such fish live, otherwise they wouldn't be so big. If there is already as much as they can eat, then heavy pre-baiting over a short period may fail. The fish will be preoccupied with natural food and your groundbait may go untouched. If the fish do feed on it, it won't take much to fill their stomachs and then they won't want your hook-bait.

If they don't want the groundbait, obviously they won't want the hook-bait either; which is exactly what happens in waters like Redmire Pool, and which may easily suggest that pre-baiting is ineffective. In such circumstances, small quantities introduced over a longer period are more likely to work, especially if, as must happen sooner or later, the pre-baiting leads up to a temporary period when natural food is in shorter supply.

18 Carp revel in weeds and mud

It's been very interesting to hear about the 28lb carp which may or may not have been taken from the Pocklington Canal.

I am not in a position to comment on the truth or otherwise of the story, but I can say definitely that there is no reason at all why a disused, weedy, and partially silted canal should not grow carp of that size, and perhaps very much larger. Lots of weeds and a fair depth of mud are just what the doctor ordered where carp are concerned, and they do not need very deep water either.

I know more than one quite small lake, everywhere less than 4ft deep, where there are carp of over 20lb, and I have seen more than one carp between 15 and 20lb in the Basingstoke Canal, usually in the weedier parts.

I notice that doubts have been expressed about the possibility of getting a really big carp out of the Pocklington Canal, on account of the heavy weed. Now, nobody ought to be scared of weed, because it is quite possible to get the biggest carp that ever swam out of the weediest water that ever existed.

It can be done in one of two ways, and the best way is to clear out some of the weed in the spot you choose to fish. Lots of anglers seem unwilling to consider any fishing in terms of more than one day; in carp fishing, it pays to think in terms of a whole summer, and the thinking can begin before the fishing. In the case of weed-problems it can begin towards the end of May, when a couple of weekends spent with a rope and a double-sided rake, clearing out openings among the growing weeds, can set the stage for dramatics in the opening days of the coarse-fishing season.

If these openings are groundbaited and kept clear through the summer, the carp will learn to frequent them. I am always hearing and reading about waters that are so heavily weeded as to be unfishable, but I have never seen one yet that couldn't be made fishable by means of an effective drag and some sweat.

If every angler confronted with excessive weed put in some time in clearing it, there would be fewer complaints about weed — and it is just as well to remember that you won't get big fish without it.

Having cleared openings, and the time having arrived to fish them, it is as well to choose tackle that will keep a hooked fish in those openings, or, failing that, give the angler a chance of getting a fish out of the weeds if it goes in.

This is where lots of people 'come unstuck', because just using a stronger line and hook is not enough. The pressure you can put on a fish is determined much more by the rod than by the line, and if you are going to use, say, a 9 or 11lb line to cope with big carp in weedy conditions, it's no good using a roach rod with it. If you haven't a proper carp rod and don't want to buy or make one, use a light pike-spinning rod, or else make or have made a short top for the lighter rod.

That is the long-term way of dealing with weed problems. The short-term way is to find where the carp are, all among the weeds, and fish for them there without any clearance at all. I've seen big carp caught among weeds so thick that you couldn't get a bait to the bottom with a 2oz lead attached to it. What one does is to use quite stout tackle — a line of 15lb bs may even be needed — and fish a floating crust in the middle of the weeds. The whole secret of dealing with big fish in weeds is to realise that the thicker the weed, the harder it is for the fish to force its way through them.

A fish in weed never travels far, and if you keep your rod well up, so as to avoid the line picking up any more weed than can be helped, it is often surprising how a big fish can be played in conditions that look impossible. Indeed, if you keep the line as tight as its strength allows, it will cut a lot of the weed and pass through. When a big carp is running in the clear, the way to turn or check him is by applying a horizontal pull, with the rod parallel to the ground.

Often, of course, a lot of weed gets caught up on the line and you eventually find your fish has stopped, practically enveloped in an enormous mass of weed that has accumulated round your line. When that happens, there are two things you can do, and which you choose depends on circumstances.

If your fish is still fairly fresh, and you want to get him on the move, or if he is among weed but there is deeper, open water nearby into which, if you can move him, he will probably run, then you can hand-line him.

Simply point the rod straight down the line, pull a yard of line off the reel so you can get the rod up quickly when the fish starts off, and then take hold of the line between butt ring and reel with your spare hand and start tugging. Be ready to let go of the line and get your rod up directly you feel the fish move. You may have to tug as hard as the strength of your line allows, but usually four or five moderate tugs will shift your fish.

However, if your fish is pretty tired, and if weeds are all around and there seems to be no hope of getting him into open water, then put on a steady strain and try to move the whole lot, fish, weed and all, towards you. Put the landing-net, which I hope is a good big one, in the water and draw the mass of weeds over it. You may have to point the rod down the line and pull really hard to get everything on the move, perhaps even walking backwards, in which case a friend with the net helps. It isn't essential, though, if you can rest the net on the bottom close to the bank, because provided the pull is steady and the weed around the fish really thick, he will come without flicking a fin.

Once the fish and his enveloping weed are on the move, however slowly, keep them moving as steadily as possible, without a jerk. Have the check of the reel 'off' and wind, pump, or walk as smoothly and steadily as you can. You will find, more often than not, that you can lift the net and collect weed, carp and all — but look out when you lift because weed is heavy and you don't want to break the net. It's probably better to pull some of the weed away before you lift the net and

70

carp from the water. You'll get a shower-bath from the outraged carp when you pull the weed clear, but you won't mind that.

I see that as well as weed, the Pocklington Canal has lily pads. Lily pads are bad, though a taut line will cut them if they aren't too thick. What do the real damage are the thick roots near the bottom; if a carp gets round one of them you can usually say goodbye to it whatever tackle you are using.

There is always a chance though, even in the most difficult conditions, and I hope future seasons will see some monster carp falling to the rods of anglers in the North.

19 How chub feed

To describe the feeding habits of the chub might seem easy, for there is very little that chub will not eat. However, the diet of chub varies greatly between different rivers, in some of which one can only wonder what there is for any fish to live upon. There is no fish that is better able to make the best of a bad river than the chub. Even in filthy rivers it manages to grow to a reasonable size. This it can do because it is what might be called a general-purpose fish. The chub has a big mouth with leathery lips, so that it can intercept food coming down the current, poke about in the bottom, turn over stones, or take surface food easily, and it has powerful throat teeth that can cope with practically anything it may find. It must have digestive organs equally efficient too, for the chub will swallow crayfish, snails, mussels, frogs, fish, insects, slugs, silkweed and anything else it can find.

When it is in a feeding mood, which it usually is, it doesn't concentrate on eating any one thing or feeding in any particular way. The exception is when very large quantities of one food are in the water — such as a heavy hatch of mayfly or a gallon or so of maggots. I think it takes more to preoccupy chub than most fish, but it does happen at times.

Not only will chub eat almost anything, but they will feed at almost any time. They are as equally greedy in bright midday sunshine as they are in complete darkness, though they do tend to move into shallower, more open water at dusk or when the water is coloured by a rise. Temperature, too, affects them far less than most fish and they will go on feeding in water too warm for any other fish but rudd. In cold conditions, chub will still bite, though below 40°F (4°C) their feeding is much reduced. In fact, no fish except the grayling feeds as keenly below 40°F as above. Because chub will feed at lower temperatures than most fish, catching them in such conditions is worth studying. So often in winter, if you want to catch a fish at all you must go after dace or chub. However, it is necessary to realise that although chub will feed at temperatures well below 40°F, they behave very differently then and tactics that would succeed in ordinary conditions may fail. In recent years, I have found that fairly small stationary bait will catch chub on days when they would not take a big bait, or any bait that moves about or goes downstream.

Another thing about chub is the way they will change their minds about what they will eat. Unlike most fish, it doesn't take a complete bellyful to make a chub decide it has had enough of one kind of food. Often, they will eat a certain amount of one food, refusing everything else, and then suddenly go right off it and begin eating something different. It is not at all uncommon to bait a swim with, say, bread-and-bran, and completely fail to get a bite on flake, paste, cheese or even bits of bread-and-bran groundbait, but to catch a few fish on worm, only to find they're full of bread-and-bran.

I often think chub have a highly developed competitive instinct, because a chub that is with others will dash at and take a bait that it wouldn't have looked at had it been on its own! Chub are often very deliberate about taking a bait that they can have a good look at first, and are likely to refuse. But being opportunists their instinct is to avoid missing anything, and a bait that is dropped just to one side of them, or over their tails, is often seized like lightning — in reasonable water temperatures, that is. Having taken a bait, they are slow to spit it out even if it isn't really eatable — they'll hang on to an artificial fly for minutes — but they will eject a bait fast enough if they feel too much tackle-drag.

It is hard to decide whether chub should be classified as shoal fish or not. They are often found in shoals, especially the smaller fish up to about 3½ or 4lb, but they have no real shoal instinct as have roach or bream. A shoal of chub is really a collection of fish that have all decided to be in the same place; they do not seem to move together or follow one another's example, except of course when alarmed. The chub is primarily an individualist, whether alone or in company.

Although there is plenty of reason for describing the chub as a greedy fish, constantly on the look-out for anything it can eat, one often finds the big chub on a heavily fished water very wary. They will pick up a legered bait, give it a little pull and drop it. Then they come up and give another little pull, and so keep on for minutes on end. Knowing if and when to strike takes experience.

Years ago I used to stay with, and fish with, the late Bill Warren, whose chub currently holds the record for the species and who caught great numbers of chub upwards of 5lb. He was adamant that it was essential to wait for a good, solid pull before tightening. However, there are good chub fishers who believe in striking instantly at the least touch. Perhaps the truth of the matter is that if you mean to wait for the good bite, you mustn't change your mind about it, and conversely, if you decide to hit everything, you mustn't be slow to do so. A chub that picks up a bait, meaning to spit it out, can be hooked if you are quick enough — provided it has the bait in its mouth.

But chub, like carp, are well able to pick up and carry a bait without taking it into their mouths at all, and so perhaps in chub fishing the safest plan is to wait for the bite about which there is no doubt at all. Also like carp, chub can swallow a bait without providing much in the way of a bite-indication, and they have throat teeth that can cut even more effectively than carp. When one is using a small dead fish as a bait, it is by no means rare, after seeing a small bob of the float or feeling a tiny tap in the line, to reel up to find only the head of the bait remaining; the body of the fish has been cut off as cleanly as you could have done it with a sharp knife. Sometimes the entire fish and your hook are both missing; that can also happen with any other bait.

For some unexplained reason, while fish such as barbel and perch do like lamprey larvae as baits, chub seem especially attracted to them. They exhibit extraordinary behaviour when

74

they take them, being extremely violent, more as if they hated lampreys and wished to kill rather than eat them. Fishing lamprey larvae for chub on the Wye, I have been smashed up, even on quite strong tackle, by the sheer violence of the take.

20 Two ways to catch a chub

There are really two entirely separate and distinct ways of catching chub. There is chub fishing and there is chub hunting.

Chub fishing is what you do on such rivers as the Severn, the Wye and the Hampshire Avon. It's true that there are places on all these rivers where you can hunt chub, but mostly you fish for them, whereas on some other waters, such as the Great Ouse and the Kennet, there are places where you can fish for chub, but mostly you hunt them.

Fishing for chub consists in long-trotting a float down, or rolling a leger across a definite swim that you expect to hold chub. You usually put in some groundbait and fish quite far off. You can't see the chub, and the chub can't see you. You expect them to be there because the swim has a reputation, or because it's the sort of swim that you know is sure to hold chub. You catch quite a few chub from that swim. That is chub fishing.

Chub hunting is altogether different. The chub you hunt is not usually in what one would call a swim at all. He's in a small hole in the reeds, or under a bush, or in a cow-drink or beneath a bridge, or lying with one of his pals over a bed of those underwater lily beds that look like cabbages. Perhaps he's gone exploring up a ditch, or is basking under some lily pads.

There's no possible doubt about his being there, as a rule, because you can see him. Give him the hundredth part of a chance, and he'll see you. Then he fades away. You have to hunt him.

There are several points to note about the chub you can see. First of all, he weighs 25 per cent less than he looks. You see him, let's say, in a small space among the lily pads. He is a colossal chub, obviously weighing every ounce of six pounds. You take a quarter of an hour to crawl to where you can cast to him without letting him know you are there. He is so big, you tremble so that you can hardly cast. You take a deep breath, steady your nerves as much as you can and make your throw.

Now, quite the usual thing to happen is that you forget to set the pick-up of the reel at 'off' and your bait hits the water 3yd out with an immense splash — scaring the chub. Or the rod flashes in the sun — scaring the chub. Or you cast 2yd wide, get hung up on a lily leaf, pull to free it, and cause an agitation — scaring the chub. You may catch up on a bit of willow herb behind, and, rising 1in to free it, scare the chub.

Those are the things that usually happen to me. You then swear, beat off the flies, wipe away the sweat and go and look for another chub.

But this time, we will suppose, nothing like that happens. Not only does the bait travel fair and true, but the chub takes it. You are dead on form, and you hit him with a drawing pull that gets his head round right away. Although he beats about among the lilies, nothing breaks and before long he is netted and on the bank. You are surprised and a little disappointed to find that he doesn't weigh 6lb. Even allowing for the notorious pessimism of spring balances, and even by jerking yours and holding it a bit sideways, you can only make him 4lb 10oz. You can hardly believe that the exercise that fish has taken has sweated more than 1½lb off him. Why, anyone could see he was easily 6lb as his head came over the landing-net. It was between then and the spring balance that the weight was lost.

The moral of all this is that if you want to hunt 6lb chub, you must find some that you are sure, when you see them in the water, cannot weigh less than 8lb. Even those, when you catch them, will never weigh more than 5lb 14oz.

I once hunted two chub that no one could doubt weighed 10lb each. No one did doubt it, except one miserable fellow who said that he didn't think the smaller of the two would go above 9½lb. I spent several weeks over those two chub and eventually found out that in the early morning they moved up to the exit of an old, ruined lock, 30yd from their usual haunt. In that position they could be reached. With the aid of some appetising-looking yellow frogs I extracted both.

They weighed 6lb 13oz and 6lb 3oz respectively.

Perhaps one of the joys of chub hunting is that you can lose so many big fish. As long as you are broken, the fish can go on weighing what it obviously did weigh when you saw it in the water. You can catch four-pounders, and lose a few six-pounders that remain for you to catch another day.

With chub fishing, it isn't the same. The fish that broke you might not have been a chub at all. It could have been a pike, or a barbel, or even a salmon, depending on where you are fishing and what the bait is. Or it could have been quite an ordinary chub, foul-hooked.

But the eight-pounder you hunted was a chub all right, and it wasn't foul-hooked because you could see it take the bait. But if chub hunting has its joys, it also has its sorrows. I sometimes wonder — for chub hunting is a hot-weather pursuit — if I do not lose as much weight as the chub seem to lose.

21 How perch feed

The perch, though very different biologically, has a good deal in common with the chub. It is an opportunist feeder, grabbing what it can, and it is partially but not completely shoal-minded.

Of course, it is not quite as broadminded as the chub about what it will eat. Tiny perch live mainly upon zoo plankton, that is, very small creatures like daphnia; larger ones eat insects and tiny fish fry, and perch upwards of about half-a-pound or so seem to live mainly on fish including their own species. They also eat worms, grubs, and other insects, and they may eat a few snails and small mussels. At any rate some get themselves caught on snail and mussel bait. They don't eat vegetable matter, and although now and then a perch gets taken on cheese or bread, and also on a dead fish, I believe they prefer, nine times out of ten, to eat something they think is alive and moving.

They are hunters, and hunters not of the tiger- or cheetah-type, but more like the wolf or even the foxhound, in that they place their trust in endurance and intelligence rather than in speed and strength. They will lie in wait for their prey when they can, and make a sudden dash at it. But if they miss they keep on chasing until they lose track or overtake whatever it is they're after. They haven't the speed of the trout or pike, but they don't give up a chase as easily. A perch will hunt a bleak or a dace clean across a wide river, chopping at its tail whenever it gets near enough, and it often succeeds in damaging the tail of its quarry enough to slow it down and so overtake it. For that reason, artificial baits and lures intended for perch should always have a trailing hook or hooks.

But the same apparent intelligence that leads a perch to use such tactics also serves to warn it, quite often, against making a fatal error. Dozens of times I have watched big perch follow a spoon or other artificial bait, in clear water, and obviously spot the deception when they've come near enough. They will also examine a worm very carefully, and, as likely as not, decide it is behaving as no proper worm ought, and therefore refuse it. I cannot resist quoting Francis Francis's description of this. He says: 'How they come up to it with all sail set, their fins extended, their spines erect, as if they meant to devour it without hesitation! And how they pause when they do come up to it, and swim gently round it, as if a worm or a minnow were an article of vertu, which required the nicest taste and consideration of a connoisseur to appreciate it properly. At length one of the boldest, taking hold of the extreme tip of the tail as timidly as a bashful young gentleman takes hold of the tip of his partner's finger when he leads her to the festive quadrille, will give it a shake. Now, if you are curious, watch your float. See how it bobs down, after a fashion that would make you think the perch must not only have swallowed the bait, but half digested it, whereas, in fact, they cannot make up their minds about it. Is it real old Chelsea, or only a modern imitation?'

The moral of all this is, that big perch are no fools in clear water and bright conditions, and you can't be too careful about proper presentation of baits. Use naturals in preference to artificials, and when spinning, have a good hook right at the tail of the bait, in line with its axis of spin.

The effects of weather upon the feeding of perch are not at all well understood — at any rate, not by me! I know they will feed quite energetically in water as low in temperature as 35°F (2°C) and I've caught them at over 2½lb in water as warm as 65°F (18°C). They seem to need plenty of oxygen, because in hot spells they are hard to tempt. In such weather, they quite often feed very actively on small fish near the surface, in the early morning at just about the time when air temperature equals water temperature. In some waters, early-morning anglers out for tench, carp or bream fix up a light spinning rod, so as to be ready to cast at once if they see small fry being chased by big perch, and some specimen perch have been taken so.

Perch don't seem to feed much in darkness or even in poor light, and to catch one after dark is very rare indeed. It does happen once in a blue moon, but I've never caught a perch in the dark, or even seen anyone else catch one then. Fishing in water that is really deep has always yielded by far the best results for me when the sun is shining. This is a winter game, of course, and all the big perch I've caught at depths of from 25 to 40ft were taken between 9am and 3pm, nine out of ten being caught between 11am and 2pm. This would seem to show that perch find their food by sight, and this their big eyes would appear to confirm.

But they seem also to have a keen sense of smell, and can detect vibrations, for in coloured water they will grab vibrating spoons that they would have refused in clear water. They will also find worms in a flood-water very quickly. I fancy they can be attracted by smells, because once, in an attempt to catch some bream, I groundbaited with a mixture of sausage rusk, bread and a gallon of oxblood, and caught a lot of good perch in a place I'd never caught any from before and have never taken any from since. Fish scales mixed into groundbait definitely attract perch, but whether by sight, by scent, or both, I cannot say with certainty.

In rivers where crayfish are found, perch eat them, and I have had a few when using crayfish as bait for chub. Of fish baits, I think a big perch would rather have a gudgeon or a very small perch than anything else, but somehow I always feel more confident when using lobworms. Out of more than fifty perch I've caught to date weighing over 3lb, nearly all were taken on big, fat worms. Notwithstanding the natural food of perch, which in the case of the big ones is almost 100 per cent fish, you'll find a lively worm one of the very best baits.

Fishing reservoirs stocked with trout has shown that tandem lures fished on fast-sinking fly lines will catch perch very effectively. Among the most successful of these is one called the Hanningfield Lure. It is tied on between No 8 long-shank hooks, joined by treble-plaited 12lb monofil nylon, with bodies of white fluorescent wool ribbed with fine silver thread. The tail consists of a big, hot-orange cock hackle, wound at the rear of the back hook and clipped to size. The throat hackle is also hot-orange cock with a small bunch of cobalt-blue hackle fibres ahead of it. The wing is white goat-hair topped with speckled turkey-tail-feather fibre; this wing must not extend beyond the tail.

The Hanningfield Lure incorporates most if not all of the recognition points of a small rudd, roach or perch, and I have found no other lure nearly so effective for perch. It also catches trout, pike and zander.

In rivers, lamprey larvae are greatly liked by perch.

22 Perch

How you rate the perch depends, I think, on how old you were when you started fishing. If you catch a six-inch perch when you are a little boy, you will have a high regard for the species for the rest of your life. I have!

Perch don't like fast water. That doesn't mean they don't live in fast rivers, but where they do, you'll find them in slow stretches, slacks and backwaters. They like sandy or gravel bottom, and they're apt to congregate near shoals of gudgeon, minnows or the fry of other species, though in some rivers they don't gather at all in summer. That is particularly true of the bigger fish, which are inclined to lead a solitary life until the first frosts of autumn, when they do shoal-up.

This isn't a hard-and-fast rule, though, because I've found quite large shoals of good-sized perch in the Hampshire Avon, and occasionally in the Wye, in summer.

Shoals tend to move about a lot, and if you find perch in a swim, there is no guarantee that they will be there next day too, especially in rivers. I think that a shoal of twenty or thirty perch of from one to three pounds or more gets through a lot of food, and when they've cleared up most of the food in one place, they move on to another. In lakes, perch seem to stay in fairly deep water (if there is any) all through the year, and in winter they're in the deepest places they can find. In the heyday of Arlesey Lake, when we used to catch lots of three-pounders and a few four-pounders, we never succeeded in summer.

Occasionally a big perch would follow a spinner, but they never actually took it, and all the big fish we caught were taken between September and mid-March, in about forty feet of water. I think that they hunt mainly by sight, because the majority were caught in the middle of the day, in winter sunshine.

Perch do, however, have a good sense of smell. I used to

have some little ones in a large aquarium, and I found that one drop of water in which worms had been washed, put into the tank, would send those perch dashing around to see where the worms were.

There isn't much of a pattern where the feeding times of perch are concerned, but what there is I will describe. I've already said that winter sunshine seems to encourage lake perch in deep water to feed. In shallower lakes, in summer, shoals of big perch often attack fry on the surface at first light, if it is going to be a fine day. This activity only lasts for a short time — ten minutes to perhaps half an hour at the outside.

The best time for catching river perch is a mild autumn day, with a fine drizzle — a cross between heavy mist and light rain — gently falling. River perch like reeds and rushes, and very often they won't venture more than a foot or so from them; thus you may well have to get your bait right up against those growths to catch any perch at all. I've seen Ken Taylor move into a swim that some other angler has fished all morning without success, and Ken has taken a dozen or more big perch, simply because he fished close up against the rushes or reeds, whereas the other angler fished three or four feet away from them.

Perch are almost entirely carnivorous. They will eat any sort of insect, crustacean or small fish and, of course, worms. They eat hardly any vegetable matter, though occasionally one takes a bit of bread. Now and then a perch will take a legered dead fish, but that is uncommon. They don't scavenge like pike.

All eight of the four-pounders I have caught, and all but a few of the three-pounders, were taken on large worms. But in recent years I've had three or four three-pounders and hundreds of two-pounders while fishing trout reservoirs with fast-sinking fly lines and large two-hook lures. Perch can be caught readily on such lures — more readily, I think, than on plugs, spoons or other things of that sort. It is important to remember that perch chase small fish, overtake them from behind and close their mouths on them, unlike trout and pike, which more often overtake their prey, then turn across its line and grab it crosswise in their jaws.

Consequently, any bait or lure which you pull through the water should have a hook right at its rear if you want to hook perch. A tassel on the treble of a spoon makes little difference to its attractiveness for pike, trout or salmon, but it makes a great improvement on its effectiveness for perch.

Stirring up mud or sand with a rake will also attract perch, particularly in rivers; a feeder stream running into a lake will likewise attract them if it increases in flow, or if you stir it up a bit. I'm not sure if the effect is first-hand or second-hand: is it the mud or stirred-up sand that attracts, or are small fish attracted which in turn draw the attention of the perch? Whichever it is, it works.

Perch aren't particularly timid fish. You don't need to be as careful not to scare them as you do with most other species. Fred J. Taylor and I once caught about twenty good perch on a sweltering-hot day on the Avon, after which it got so hot that, as there were no other anglers around to disturb, and with Colonel Crow's permission, we dived in for a swim. Colonel Crow was so rash as to bet that this would put paid to our perch catching, so I reached up and took my rod from the bank, and caught another perch while up to my armpits in the water — water that Fred and I had been swimming through not two minutes before. Mind you, I was stirring up the bottom with my toes while I trotted my tackle downstream — and it didn't have to go far.

Perch have a habit of swallowing your bait if you give them half a chance, so don't. Every year, too many perch are killed through swallowing anglers' baits. You don't need to give them time, once you detect a bite. If you miss, be sure that was a little perch that you wouldn't want to catch anyway. The only exception to this is if you are legering in very deep water at long range. Then you get positive runs and you can let several yards of line run out before you tighten up.

But I've given up catching perch from great depths as I think the change of pressure does so much damage that few survive even when released. I don't condemn other anglers for doing it, but I know I've done enough myself. If I ever change my mind about that, and do it again, I'll bring my hooked fish up very slowly, taking ten or fifteen minutes over it, so they have time to adapt.

Perch are excellent fish to eat, especially those from rivers. I used to eat one or two perch every year, but in recent times perch have been dreadfully affected by disease in many of our waters, so I'll let them recover before I eat any more. However, even before the outbreak of disease, I think perch were declining in numbers. They are very susceptible to pollution, which is a pity, because the perch is a splendid fish, and nothing I've ever caught has pleased me so much as a four-pound perch. They aren't spectacular fighters — though they can tug pretty hard — but when a really big one comes up, all barred and beautiful, with its back fin erect, there are few sights in all angling to compare with it.

23 How eels feed

I have listed the things upon which perch feed. The eel eats almost exactly the same things — insects, crustaceans and fish, and, of course, whatever worms it can find — but it has very different methods of getting them.

Although eels can swim very quickly when they want to, their eyes are small and probably not efficient enough for active hunting. So when they're after live foods — and that is what they mostly eat — they rely on a stealthy approach and a quick grab. I am convinced they locate their food far more by using their sense of smell than by any other means. There is no doubt that they have this sense very well developed indeed and there are plenty of cases where they have been observed using it most effectively.

There are some curious ideas about what eels eat and what effects their feeding habits have on a fishery. Like most anglers, I took for granted what I was told about the eel — what a menace it was, how much spawn, especially salmon and trout eggs it ate, and so on — until I began thinking for myself about the matter. Now I've changed my mind somewhat. I don't think eels eat much game-fish spawn, because they're not very active at the time it's deposited. They certainly eat quite a lot of coarse-fish spawn, but is that bad?

We're always being told we must preserve pike, otherwise there will be too many other fish for the food supply, and they won't grow to worthwhile size. We have bylaws that make us return small fish, but we may kill the big ones. We preserve pike, that can eat big fish, but which eat nothing like as many small ones as eels do; they don't eat spawn at all, while eels eat plenty of it. Yet anglers seem agreed that pike should be returned alive, but every eel caught should be killed!

For the angler who wants to catch eels, knowing how they

find and take their food is much more important than accurate knowledge of their diet, because baits that are effective at any time when eels are feeding are well known. You need nothing more than lobworms or some dead fish to catch eels. For the big eels, I don't think there is a better bait than a freshly killed roach or dace, unless its a dead trout about five-inches long or a piece of trout liver. In what follows, I shall recommend waiting, after an eel has taken a dead-fish bait, until it has run, stopped, and then started to move off again. But in some waters, to follow this advice would mean losing the eel through its having taken refuge under rocks, waterlogged timbers or discarded bedsteads. This is where trout liver, or failing that, liver from other fish, is useful. It allows immediate striking when a bite is detected.

Remembering that the eel's sense of smell is what helps it most to find its food, a dead-fish bait should be pricked all over, or cut about with a knife, so that its juices may be smelled by the eels from far away. Eels seldom feed other than at the bottom, so the bait should be there.

Now, every eel knows that if it can smell food, plenty of other eels must have smelt it too, so it makes for the food as quickly as it can. But not in a mad rush, for it doesn't know yet if the food is dead or alive, and if alive, the eel doesn't want to scare it; thus it approaches quickly but craftily. Once it has found the bait, the eel knows that other eels who have scented it won't be long in arriving, so it makes off just as fast as it can move, putting a good distance between itself and its friends before it stops to swallow. Of course, if the bait is small and the eel big, it may swallow it immediately, but with a five-inch-fish bait and a two-or three-pound eel, the swallowing process takes time, and the eel doesn't want to lose half the fish to one of its brothers or sisters. So, when using a dead-fish bait, never strike until a biting eel moves off for the *second* time, if you want to make quite sure of hooking your fish.

Like all fish, eels are affected by water temperature and aren't very active below about 50°F (10°C), though they are caught now and then in much colder water. I never knew the temperature to be too high for eels to feed, though. In fact, for daytime eel fishing, I don't think it can be too warm. I've caught lots of big eels on sweltering-hot days when hardly any other fish would bite except small rudd. Thus I think it must be the waning light of evening, and not the fall in water temperature usually accompanying it that causes eels to feed more freely at that time.

Eels will feed, of course, in bright sunshine or complete darkness, but there is no doubt that they feed most freely from dusk to dawn. In fact, they're the only British fish about which it can be truly said at all times that all-night fishing is very much more productive than all-day fishing. There may be exceptions to this, but I've never met them. Eels also move in near to the banks after dark, when long casting becomes unnecessary.

Since eels have so keen a sense of smell, it is possible to attract them very easily. Such things as blood, minced kipper, chickens' or rabbits' guts, will bring them round. I have read that breaking an egg in the water will also attract eels from a long way off. The other day I blew an egg — a swan's — for a young lady. It had been floating in the water for some time. I should think its contents might well have attracted eels. They certainly attracted flies and comments, but they did not greatly attract me, which brings me to the old argument about whether eels prefer a fresh or a stinking fish to eat. I don't know the answer to that one. Eels will eat fish either fresh or stinking, but I have never known stinking ones do better as bait than fresh ones, and as the latter are more pleasant to handle, I prefer to use them; I don't think I catch fewer eels as a result.

The diet of eels varies to some extent, depending upon the water in which they live. Now, eels are nice to eat but, as with other animals, just how nice depends upon how they've fed. If you want the very best fresh-water eels to eat, find a clean river where the eels can get plenty of fresh-water shrimps. I know one where every eel you catch has its belly full of fresh-water shrimps, and the flesh of these eels is as pink as that of a salmon. I am almost as concerned about how I feed as I am about how fish feed, and I wouldn't exchange a dish of those pink-fleshed eels for any other kind of fish you could offer me. Not even fresh salmon.

24 You need hefty tackle for big eels

Let me make another appeal on behalf of the eel. The eel is a fish capable of providing splendid sport, and it is one of the best fish there is to take home and cook.

In fact, it's the only fish worth cooking that every angler can fish for and take home without getting into trouble for not returning it.

It fights with terrific power, and usually gives you two fights — one in the water and one on the bank; and the record for the species is wide open to be broken. The freeze-up proved that; quite a number of eels were found dead that would have easily broken the present record if they'd been caught on rod and line.

Big eels aren't difficult to hook. In some waters, especially lakes and ponds, they bite best on dead fish; in rivers, a bunch of lobworms sometimes does better, or if a fish is used, it is sometimes best to use quite a small one, like a gudgeon. I keep saying 'sometimes' because you may need to experiment to find the best bait.

If you are after monster eels, it will pay you to use a foot or so of wire between your hook and the running line, joining the two with a swivel.

It will also pay you to use strong tackle — if I expected to hook a 10lb eel I'd use tackle at least as strong as I'd choose for a 40lb carp, and probably that wouldn't be strong enough!

However, for general big-eel fishing, something like a Mk IV carp rod or a salmon spinning rod, with a 10lb or 12lb line, does quite well.

You also need a hook that is strong in the wire, and completely reliable in temper. I think a single hook is best, with a straight eye. Sharpen it!

It's a good idea to prepare half-a-dozen or more baits in advance if you're using dead fish. Deflate the swim-bladders and thread each bait on the wire trace so that the hook is at the mouth of the bait and the wire comes out at the root of the tail. Then attach a swivel to each, which is easy with Alasticum wire.

If you decide to use nylon instead of wire, pinch a big shot on at the bait's tail, to keep it from sliding up the trace. An eel with his mouth bunged up with the bait can't bite your nylon so easily and the shot stops the bait being ejected, once the eel is hooked.

If, however, a record eel is your ambition, then I advise you to use wire, and strong wire at that. A 20lb single wire will do — I've known eels bite clean through the stranded wire that is generally used for single pike hooks or snap-tackles.

One more piece of equipment — landing gear. After trying various ingenious devices, like spiked tongs, barbed gaffs etc, I've come to the conclusion that the best thing to use is the biggest landing-net you can get. My 36in carp landing-net would cope with the biggest eel in Britain. You can buy a 32in net that will be fine for your record eel.

Where to find these monsters? Well, they can be almost anywhere, but if you can find a pond, lake or pit that is within a few hundred yards of a river or stream, you can bet there will be eels in it; and if the lake teems with undersized roach or rudd, you can depend on it that some of the eels will be monsters. A great many of Britain's biggest eels live in ponds that anglers consider not worth fishing. Lots of little fish are what eels need to grow big.

The best time to fish for eels? Through a warm night — but there is no time when they won't bite, and I've caught plenty around 4lb in the middle of sweltering-hot days. They like it warm, and if it's dark too, they like it better still.

Rivers hold big eels, and in those you need lead if there is much current. Often, you can't let river eels run too far with a bait because of weeds or snags, and you can't let them run on the open spool of a fixed-spool reel as the current will have all your line out if the eel doesn't.

92

That's why you may have to use worms in rivers, or small fish. You can strike earlier with smaller baits. In reasonably weed-free still waters, however, you can use dead fish up to 3oz or even 4oz, and then you let the eel run till he stops, without check; after he has stopped you wait till he has started to move off second time, before you strike.

When he is hooked, don't try to play him as you would other fish. Pull as hard as the tackle will stand and keep on pulling. Don't expect to play him out — keep him coming and net him at the first chance. Then get him well back from the water before you shake him from the net into a sack.

Don't attempt to get the hook out — cut the line and attach a ready-baited trace for the next eel. You can tie up your sack and put it in the water to keep your eels alive.

If you don't fancy eating your catch, you shouldn't find it difficult to find plenty of people who will be glad of it, including your local fishmonger. He'll probably buy it!

Did you know that smoked eel and smoked salmon are about the same price?

25 How pike feed

Now I come to a fish about which there is much argument —
the pike. It eats any animal matter it can profitably get. Dead
or alive, fish, fowl, mammal, insect or crustacean, it's all the
same to the pike. It will eat whatever provides the biggest meal
for the amount of energy needed to get it. In fact, the main
item in the diet of pike is fish — any kind of fish — and it is
probable that the pike eats more dead fish than is commonly
supposed.

But while a pike will eat any fish, dead or alive, it has its
preferences. Trout and grayling are greatly preferred to roach,
rudd, bream, carp, chub or perch. Sea fish, too, can be
attractive: a mackerel or a piece of one is as appealing to pike as
trout or grayling, and a herring runs it close. Eels are also more
of a favourite than is generally assumed, and a piece of one
makes a good bait.

Other things being equal, a pike prefers the biggest fish it
can comfortably swallow. But since other things are not always
equal, big pike are often found to have eaten a lot of small fish,
while every angler knows that big pike are frequently taken on
small baits. There are reasons for this. Sometimes, when small
fish are in dense shoals, pike can grab them in numbers at one
mouthful. And while a pike of 20lb may prefer a 2lb roach to a
two-ouncer, it doesn't mind snapping up a two-ouncer (or an
artificial bait that seems like a two-ouncer) if it almost bumps it
on the nose.

As regards the conditions in which they will feed, it is
difficult to lay down any definite rules, but the old idea that icy
conditions favour pike fishing is not borne out by my own
experience, and I would say that water temperatures below
about 40°F (4°C) are as unfavourable for pike fishing as they
are for fishing of any other kind.

Warm conditions, on the other hand, only seem to worry

pike if they severely reduce the amount of oxygen dissolved in the water. Pike, like other predatory fish, need
plenty of oxygen and in cases of the sort of pollution that
reduces dissolved oxygen, pike are among the first to
suffer.

Another factor that is against successful pike fishing is
muddy water. I don't say pike can't be caught when the river is
shifting a lot of mud and silt; I do say that I've always found it
much harder to catch them when it is.

There seems also to be a tendency on the part of pike to feed
very heavily and then to fast for several days at a time. That, at
any rate, is the impression that regular pike fishers get. But it is
noticeable that on those days when pike seem right off, if one *is*
hooked, it is very often a whopper. It may be, therefore, that
when thirty-pounders are on a feeding spree, smaller pike
wisely lie low. A pike of 30lb can swallow anything, including
another pike weighing up to 10lb.

Pike hunt by scent, sight and by detecting vibrations, and, as
everyone knows, catch their food either by lying in ambush, or
after approaching slowly and stealthily, by making a sudden
short rush at terrific speed.

They can be attracted by groundbait containing blood
and/or fish scales, or by minced-up sprats or herrings. A
vibrating spinner attracts their attention, but I have small faith
in artificials except for use in coloured water. That very keen
eyesight, which helps pike catch real fish, can distinguish all
too clearly between a roach and a bit of painted tin or wood.
When pike are not feeding, they can be stimulated into
grabbing a bait if it is brought past them time after time. If you
see a good pike and it refuses your bait, don't give up. Keep on
bringing the bait past its nose, and sooner or later it will strike
— except perhaps in March, when it may be concerned with
spawning, and then nothing will attract it.

It is curious how a pike will sometimes lie in the middle of a
shoal or roach or other fish, without making any attempt to
catch one of them. They seem to know the pike won't attack

them, and swim all around it quite fearlessly. Yet that same pike will instantly seize a livebait dropped in front of it. I don't understand why this should be. Some say pike have an instinct to eat sick or injured fish. This I emphatically refuse to believe. It may be that roach know to a nicety how much energy that pike is willing to expend on catching one of them, or just how fast it can move after them — for the pike cannot swim backwards, nor can it strike accurately on the turn. Watch a pike preparing to attack, and you will see that it has to go through a most complicated process of aiming its body at the intended prey, unless it happens to be dead ahead of the pike. Free, healthy roach probably take care not to get dead ahead of a pike they can easily see.

Anyone who has seen how slow pike often are in deciding to take a bait, and how long they take to aim themselves at it once they have chosen to take it, must realise that searching the water with spinning tackle is a relatively inefficient method of pike fishing, likely to be successful only on those days when the pike are feeding much more freely than usual.

In the ordinary way, very many more pike see the spinner than ever take it — yet a lot of these pike could be caught on a bait that remained near them long enough. I believe that the man who knows exactly where to find pike will catch many more by using live or dead baits than by spinning. But such baits cannot succeed unless they are put where pike can find them, whereas a spinner may find an odd pike energetic enough to grab it. Therefore, if pike seem to be feeding heartily, spin — preferably with a real fish and not an artificial bait — especially if the water is clear.

If they aren't feeding freely, use your knowledge and common sense to decide the likeliest place for a good pike to be, and then put a fish on snap-tackle in that place and give the pike plenty of time to think over the matter of whether it shall take it or not. The pike may decide in the affirmative. In choosing a spot, remember that in rivers and canals, there are twenty times as many pike within a yard of the bank than there are in the rest of the water — unless someone has scared them out.

It is worth knowing that there *are* times when even the largest pike prefers a bunch of big worms to anything else you can offer it, but under what conditions this applies, I am unable to say with certainty.

The view is quite widely held that pike feed little on days following bright, moonlit nights, as they have fed by moonlight. Why pike should choose moonlight in preference to daylight, I cannot think. I have never caught a pike at night, nor seen one caught, whether there was moonlight or not. My experience is that they feed mainly in broad daylight. Very early morning, or late evening, are not their feeding times, though these fish are occasionally taken then. Moonlit nights are always chilly, and a fall in water temperature seems a more probable explanation for pike not feeding very freely the next day.

Pike will sometimes take baits that they have not the slightest intention of swallowing, and very exasperating it can be, especially when livebaiting. After the float has gone under and away, up it bobs again. You think the pike has stopped to turn the bait, strike after due pause and find the pike has dropped it, after all. On such days you get far more runs and far fewer fish than usual, even if you try striking immediately. The same happens in carp fishing now and then, and, to a less noticeable extent, with other species. Don't ask me what to do about it; I don't know.

26 Groundbaiting for pike

We were fishing a Hertfordshire stream that runs into the Lea. Fred Taylor was after pike and I was after roach. Fred threw in about thirty sprats, as groundbait, and cast out another sprat on leger tackle.

I don't suppose you have ever heard of groundbaiting for pike with sprats before, have you? I hadn't anyway, and I must admit I hadn't a lot of faith in it. But after a while, Fred had a bite on his leger, struck, and hooked a pike. He played it for a time and then it bit through his tackle. He wasn't using wire.

I'm always reading books and articles in which the authors say that wire isn't necessary for pike as they invariably use nylon and very seldom lose a fish. Blessed if I know how they manage it, because whenever I try to catch pike without wire, I lose nearly every fish I hook. The only ones I land are the unlucky ones that get hooked right at the edge of the jaw so that all the nylon is outside the mouth.

Well, away went Fred's pike with Fred's hook in it. I carried on roach fishing. After a couple of hours I couldn't get any more bites, and then a small roach skipped out of the water and I thought probably a pike had got into my swim. So I fixed up a pike rod, some 12lb line and a paternoster tackle with a treble hook on a bit of wire. I put on the smallest roach I had in the keep-net, a half-pounder, and dropped it in.

It was taken straight away, and having given the pike time to turn the bait, I tightened up and hooked it. It didn't take much playing, as it was only about three pounds, and it was soon on the bank. In that river the rule is that all pike are killed. Most of the water is preserved as a trout fishery, and they have been killing pike every way they can think of, as often as possible, for at least fifty years, without the roach and dace getting too small or too numerous. In fact I don't know any water in Britain that holds better roach and dace, and in spite of all that is done, there are still plenty of pike. So we killed the one I'd caught, and cut it open to see what was inside. I found Fred Taylor's hook and seven sprats.

That fish had shovelled up seven sprats from the bottom, been hooked and played, got off, then went about seventy yards upstream and grabbed a half-pound roach. I expect some other pike had also been eating the sprats and had cleared up the lot. The one I caught was still hungry with seven inside, so he'd wandered off to see what else he could find to eat.

It shows that groundbaiting for pike is effective in attracting them. Fred says that pieces of fish are just as good, it doesn't have to be whole sprats. There is no doubt that pike are perfectly willing to pick up dead fish, or pieces of dead fish, from the bottom, and that you can fish for pike in exactly the same way as you would for tench, bream, carp etc, throwing in groundbait and legering (or float fishing if you like) in the groundbaited area. Thus it isn't necessary for the bait to be alive or even to appear to be alive. The bait can be fresh-water fish or sea fish, and still effectively catch pike, very often indeed. I say very often, because we have found that sometimes the pike won't look at a dead bait, but will take a live bait or a spinner. There are also times when they'll have a spinner and refuse a live bait, and I've known a pike refuse to take the least notice of a spinner, but grab a live bait directly it saw it. No one knows what governs these preferences.

But from what I've seen during the last twenty years, a dead bait is as likely as anything to catch a pike, whether it's in a river or still water, and I suspect there are plenty of times when pike are too lethargic to move after a live, or apparently live, bait, but will slide up slowly and take a dead one. What's more, they can be attracted with fish groundbait, and that's a method I am going to try more often in future. I think it will produce results.

One thing that has to be avoided is pike swallowing the bait. No one wants to hook a pike in the guts, least of all Fred

Taylor, but it happened with his fish although he struck quite soon. There is a definite tendency for pike that have picked up a dead fish to swallow it right away. With a live one, they probably chew it up a bit to kill it, but a dead one goes 'down the hatch' immediately.

For that reason, I suggest we should use two trebles in a dead bait and strike instantly if we get a run.

27 How trout feed

In discussing the feeding of trout, we find ourselves in a somewhat curious position, since on most waters holding these fish only the artificial fly may be used, and we cannot use as bait the various things that trout eat, which include worms, small fish, water snails and other animals.

They also eat insects, of course, and where these are plentiful they form the greatest part of the diet of the trout, being eaten in larvae and pupae form even more than when winged. It is this that has given rise to the art of fly fishing, and while the purpose of this book is to explain what fish eat and how they obtain their food, I have to digress somewhat in dealing with trout to talk about angling methods as well.

The reasons why only fishing with the artificial fly is allowed on so many trout waters are rather complex. There can be no doubt that, once an angler has become reasonably proficient in the art of fly fishing, it is the most enjoyable way of catching trout. I will go farther: a standard of ability in fly fishing can be reached that makes it not only the most enjoyable but also the most successful method to use on most if not all waters.

It is not, however, the easiest method for the beginner. The motivations behind the fly-only rule are, first, that those who are good enough to find it the most enjoyable method are anxious that others should learn the art and thus share the pleasure, a worthy motive. But second, if on many of our waters bait fishing were to be permitted, numbers of anglers too lazy or too stupid to learn fly fishing, would be able to pull out as many trout as the skilful fly fishers, greatly increasing the total catch and thus stocking costs, leading in turn to massive increases in day and season-ticket prices.

There are rivers and streams holding trout where no restrictions are placed on methods and the angler may, if he wishes, spin or fish with baits like minnows, worms and natural insects. On such waters, the angler needs only to know that trout do not shoal; each finds its own territory in which it feeds when it can. A trout will drive smaller fish from its chosen territory; if it is caught, its territory will be quickly occupied by another trout nearly as large.

The species of trout native to Britain is the brown trout. It differs from the introduced rainbow trout in that it has a longer life, slower growth, and, as it increases in size, a much greater tendency to eat more small fish and fewer other foods like insects. In some Scottish and Irish lochs, brown trout reach weights of 20lb and more, living almost entirely on other fish including their own species. For these, fly fishing is wellnigh useless, the usual method of angling for them being to trail a spinner of some kind, either artificial or a real fish on a spinning tackle, behind a boat. A lure made of hair or feathers may be substituted for the spinner, but that does not really make the method fly fishing.

Rainbow trout differ from brown trout not only in their eating fewer small fish and more foods of other kinds but also in their tolerance of higher water temperatures, and conversely, intolerance of very cold water. I cannot give specific temperatures because the behaviour of both species of fish varies from one water to another, but in general, rainbows will continue to feed in water several degrees warmer than the level at which brown trout have ceased to feed. Brown trout will go on feeding in water too cold for rainbows to do so.

In artificial waters — which range from water-supply reservoirs having great depths and areas of hundreds of acres to small lakes of from one to thirty acres or so — the main foods of rainbow trout and also of brown trout up to about four-years-old are daphnia, midge pupae (often called buzzer nymphs) and water snails. They also eat other creatures: sedge flies and their caddises, corixae, damsel, dragonfly and water-beetle larvae, and various ephemeridae where present, like pond and lake olives, sepia and claret duns, and caenis. However, examination of stomach contents shows that the greater part of their growth is made on the first three organisms I have mentioned, at any rate in the more fertile waters.

Both kinds of trout also eat land insects when the opportunity occurs, including daddy longlegs, ladybirds, flying ants, drone flies and small beetles. On some waters, members of the *Bibio* family, black gnats, hawthorn flies and heather flies are found on the surface and eaten, as are various terrestrial moths.

It is important to realise that daphnia, in the richer waters, constitute so high a proportion of trout diet because these tiny crustaceans perform vertical migrations daily, the depth at which they are found being governed mainly by light intensity. In the dark they are at or very near the surface; on a bright sunny day and in clear water, they may be as deep as thirty feet or more. Not only do trout tend to follow these migrations, except when some other and usually larger organism provides a counter-attraction; small fish of other species, where present, follow the daphnia too, and they in turn attract the big, predatory brown trout.

In rivers and in some of the more acid lakes, daphnia and midge pupae are largely replaced by ephemerids like mayflies, olive duns, iron-blue duns, pale wateries, blue-winged olives, and of course the still-water ephemerids already mentioned. Sedge flies and their larvae, caddis grubs, are also eaten together with a wide range of terrestrial insects whenever these get on the water.

I have explained earlier in this book how fish can become preoccupied with eating a particular kind of food which happens to be present in large quantities. Of no fish is this more apparent than with trout, probably because much of their food consists of small creatures which make their appearance in large numbers, all at about the same time.

The pupae or nymphs of various insects rise to the surface to transpose into their winged forms; flights of flying ants, or numbers of land insects like ladybirds and drone flies fall on the water in quantity; the water snails make collective ascents to the surface, and so on. Thus we find trout at times feeding on one kind of creature and ignoring all others, and it is the frequency with which this happens that makes fly fishing so fascinating. It forces the angler to use, and perhaps devise and tie, a fly that the trout will mistake for a real insect of the kind they are eating. To make the most of fly fishing, an angler should learn to invent and tie his own flies. Of course he can buy a wide selection, but if he does that, he deprives himself of some of the pleasure of the method.

In order to devise successful imitative artificial flies, an angler must understand not only the optical equipment of a trout but also how its rather limited brain works. A trout can see all the colours we see and probably some that we cannot, especially in the area of infra-red. It can see very clearly at near and long range, and all in between. Its ability to interpret what it sees is, fortunately for anglers, very limited, however. Generally speaking, if in an artificial fly a trout can see two or three points of resemblance to the real insect that fly is trying to imitate, then the trout will ignore quite flagrant points of difference, like a large bend, barb and point of a hook, or a hundred 'legs' in the artificial fly where the real one has but six. Indeed, if this were not so, it would be impossible to catch a trout on an artificial fly when a particular kind of food was engaging its entire attentions.

The angler, however, has to look at the real insect or other creature that the trout is eating, and try to judge which if its features are those by which the trout recognises it; if he can incorporate these features, or at least some of them, in his artificial fly then he has a good chance of catching the fish, especially if he remembers that recognition points may not only be visual but also behavioural. In other words, it is no good having a fly that looks right if it moves (or fails to move when it should) in a way different from the real insect.

I must qualify the above, though, by saying that there is good reason to suppose that a judicious exaggeration of a point of recognition or a form of movement, or both, can add to the attraction of an artificial fly. Trout are not, however, always feeding selectively, and when they are not, they may be induced to take artificial flies that excite their curiosity, resentment or hunger.

Selectively feeding or preoccupied trout are commonly found at or near the surface and betray their presence there by one or another kind of disturbance, so that they are not hard to locate. Trout that are not feeding selectively are often deeper and much more difficult to find. Consequently, while the selective feeders pose a more difficult problem in choice of fly, the others demand greater exercise of watercraft and general angling knowledge. Clearly, the most successful angler is he who can adapt to meet every circumstance.

Among the fly patterns often used on large reservoirs are what have come to be called lures: large concoctions of hair or feather dressed either on a single large hook, or two or three hooks arranged in tandem. These are said to give the impression of small fish, and so they may, but it is equally likely that trout take them out of curiosity, or resentment of what appears to be an intruder in their territory. However that may be, it is worth knowing that a trout's method of attack upon a fast-moving lure, spinner, or small fish, is to overtake it at one side or the other, and then to turn across its track and grab it at the head end. This form of attack differs from that employed by perch, which attack from behind, snapping at the tail end, probably in an attempt to cripple and slow down the small fish, or what they think is one.

There are times when trout, like other fish, will attack a fly, and particularly one of these large lures, quite differently. They have no intention of eating it, and they nip at part of the dressing without taking the hook or hooks into their mouths, just as a carp or chub will sometimes run off with a ball of paste, or a boiled potato, holding it in such a way that the hook fails to gain a hold. This kind of behaviour on the part of trout is known as 'coming short' and for more than a hundred years its cause and cure have been discussed by anglers. Various expedients, like small, treble hooks trailing behind the lure, or lures dressed short on a long-shank hook, have been tried, but without any real success. Neither unorthodox arrangements of hooks nor bad language will help; all that one can do is wait patiently until the fish begin to take properly, which they usually do if given time.

When trout are feeding at or near the surface, generally on insects, the form their movements take can often help the angler to decide what they are eating. A newly hatched insect on the surface is usually taken with a very positive chomp that can easily be seen and heard. On the other hand, insects that have returned to the water and laid their eggs, like the spinners of the various ephemerid flies, are taken with little disturbance and a sound like a tiny kiss. Midge pupae are eaten methodically, the trout usually working upwind, breaking the surface with their mouths and usually showing the upper lobes of the tail fin as they resume an even keel. The appearance of a calm patch in a ripple indicates that a trout below has turned to intercept a rising nymph, pupa, or corixa coming up for air. In a wave, this movement produces what has been called a 'shatter' effect, as if an area of water had been suddenly flattened with a table-tennis bat. When caenis are on the water in large numbers, the surface is nearly always calm and the trout swim around with their noses breaking the surface, gobbling up the insects and pursuing an erratic course. Otherwise, when there is plenty of surface or near-surface food, trout tend to travel very straight upwind, feeding as they go. When they reach an area where there is less food, they go down to a depth of about six feet and swim rapidly back to their starting point, seldom taking anything until they reach that point and have returned to near the surface, headed upwind again.

For some reason that I have never heard satisfactorily explained, strips of calm water sometimes form on lakes. They are known variously as slicks, calm lanes, scum lanes or wind lanes; they run in line with the wind and cut through rippling water. Their presence may be due to alteration in surface tension caused by concentrations of algae or some other cause. In suitable conditions they can be easily produced by putting a few drops of oil on the surface.

A lane produced artificially seems to have no attraction for trout, but one having a natural origin most certainly has, and trout feed freely both in the calm lane and in the ripple adjacent to it on each side. Far more often than not, it is midge pupae that they eat in such a lane and it is not impossible that it is these pupae that actually produce, in the process of hatching, some substance that changes the surface tension sufficiently for the lane to be formed.

It will be obvious that when trout are feeding on an up-wind course, a fly or flies drawn across or partly across the wind will cover more fish than one cast and retrieved straight downwind. Not only will it cross the line of movement and therefore be seen by more fish; it will also be seen in side view, and because of its line of movement, more likely to hook any fish that takes it.

It remains to say that very large brown trout, feeding almost entirely on fish, feed less frequently and for shorter periods than smaller trout living on small food items. The large lake trout and the big trout — of which a few still inhabit the Thames and some other rivers — may feed just twice every day, and for only long enough to catch and swallow two or three fish weighing up to half a pound each. Obviously a great deal of observation and study is necessary to catch trout of this kind consistently. However, with trout of all sorts, an angler may always feel optimistic; as I have often heard it said, 'there is always a fool' and even in the most discouraging circumstances, a trout bent on suicide may find the angler offering the opportunity for it to do so.

28 Study the trout's favourite grub

You don't need to know the names of all the insects on which trout feed, but it is useful to know something about how the different sorts develop and behave. Let me give you an example to illustrate why it pays to know something about insects.

Members of one family of water insects are called sedge flies, or sedges for short. They come in various sizes and colours. Nearly all of them start off in the familiar form of a caddis grub and then rise to the surface of the water as a swimming pupa. Once there they emerge into a winged form, looking rather like a moth with long antennae or 'horns', but with the wings, when folded, making an angle or ridge rather like a house roof instead of nearly flat as in a true moth.

These sedges are lively little insects. As soon as they have emerged from their pupal form, they want to get airborne, so they practise take-off runs, scuttling along the surface, sometimes for yards. Then they rest a while and try again, until they eventually take off, fly to the bank, and alight on grass, reeds, or bushes. Consequently, when you are using an artificial fly that imitates a winged sedge, you want it to sit well up on the surface of the water, and having cast it out, be able to retrieve it in a series of fast pulls, with rests in between, skimming it over the surface in imitation of the real thing.

Now consider the daddy longlegs: its grub, called a leather-jacket, lives among grass roots. In due course it changes to a pupa from which, in turn, the winged insect hatches. For some unaccountable reason, numbers of daddies decide to fly across water, and if the water is wide, very few of them reach the other side. They tire, fall on the water, and lie there inert with their legs trailing. They can't swim; the best they can manage is a few dying twitches.

If you fish with an artificial daddy longlegs and skim it across the surface as you would an artificial sedge fly, you'll catch few, if any, trout. You may find that trout will follow it, say for twenty yards, if you drag it across or through the water but they won't often take it. Perhaps they are curious as to why a daddy longlegs, which they know as a feeble creature, should suddenly become possessed of phenomenal swimming power. They are also suspicious of any daddy longlegs that sits on the water with its legs spread out all around as it would on land, because the real thing ought to have its legs trailing when it goes into the water. So, you must dress the artificial with trailing legs and, having cast it out, let it lie motionless until either a trout takes it, or wind and drift make it necessary to cast again.

That is one example of how knowledge of the behaviour of two different insects enables the angler to design and fish the artificials in the way that will catch most trout.

Obviously, I haven't space in this chapter to describe the life-cycle and habits of all the numerous insects you find at the waterside. For those who want to know more, I can recommend three excellent books. They are as follows:

An Angler's Entomology, J. R. Harris (Collins)
Trout Fly Recognition, John Goddard (A. & C. Black)
Trout Flies of Still Water, John Goddard (A. & C. Black)

You should be able to borrow these from your local public library, but I would advise buying some or all of them if you can afford it, especially if you tie your own flies, because each of these books is well illustrated in colour, and you will want to refer to them often.

Another very useful exercise consists in collecting insects. My bag always has room in it for three or four small, transparent plastic pill-bottles in which I can put any interesting insects I find at the waterside. I also have a small aquarist's fine-mesh net which John Goddard gave me, adapted so that it can be attached to a landing-net handle. It is invaluable for catching nymphs, pupae and other water creatures, and I've learned a lot from the things I've caught with it.

When you are designing flies, there is nothing like hanging your artificial in a jam-jar, in which some of the real insects are sculling about. You can learn how the real thing and the artificial compare, in the conditions in which the trout will be comparing them, namely in or on the water. I also possess a plastic basin with a hole cut in the bottom, into which a piece of glass has been fitted, so that I can examine insects and artificial flies from below. This is a very useful thing to have and not very difficult to make.

Beginners at trout fishing are understandably puzzled by all the different artificial flies they see in the shops and in other anglers boxes and are apt to ask for 'suggested lists of killing patterns', charts showing which pattern to use in each month of the season, and so on. Or else they pin their faith in fancy patterns that don't imitate anything in particular but which they have heard are successful.

You can fish the same fly, one single pattern and size, all season if you like, and you will probably catch some fish, but you won't catch nearly as many as you will if you study real insects and choose, or better still tie yourself, artificials resembling them.

29 Salmon, sea trout, zander and other fish

Salmon and sea trout

The authorities are unanimous in saying that salmon and sea trout do not feed in fresh water. In the sense that they do not take in much food there, and may not be able to digest what they do take and swallow, this is true. It is manifestly untrue, however, that they never take or swallow food in fresh water, as anyone who has caught salmon or sea trout on worms can tell you. Salmon, given time, swallow worms right down to their guts and sea trout often do the same. Both species will also, at times, rise methodically to surface insects just like trout, and they may then be caught on imitative artificial flies.

What seems to happen is this: salmon and sea trout that have just arrived in a river have the memory of sea feeding firmly imprinted on their minds and are then likely to grab, from force of habit, anything that resembles what they have been eating in the sea; usually, small fish. Devon minnows, spoon baits and large flies or lures that resemble small fish are likely to be taken then. After some time in the river, and also as the water becomes warmer, the fish remember their lives as parr, before they migrated to sea and were feeding on fresh-water insects, crustacea and other organisms. Then the fish-simulating lure is less attractive and the fly that gives the impression of an insect may become more so. So too is the natural shrimp; no doubt every salmon and sea trout became familiar with fresh-water shrimps at its parr stage.

The main difference, apart from size, between salmon and sea trout is that salmon take best in daylight, if they take at all, whereas sea trout take best after dark. That is only a general rule, but it is true as such. However, the fact that these fish do not feed in a true sense in fresh-water limits what I can say about them here.

Zander

The behaviour of zander is relatively simple. In general they tend to be nocturnal, though muddy or coloured water, by reducing light, has much the same effect as darkness. Their response to water temperature is similar to that of perch, as is their ability to locate potential prey by scent and vibration, though, we have reason to think, far less by sight. They eat fish, any sort of fish, and as yet we have little evidence that they prefer one sort to another. They will also take worms, and they are sometimes taken on artificial spinners or tandem lures, as are perch.

Where there are plenty of small fish like roach, rudd, dace or bream, shoals of zander can be attracted, as can pike, by groundbaiting to attract and hold the small fish. The vibrations the small fish produce in their feeding are readily detectable by predatory species.

Zander are said to grab their prey fish by the belly and this they frequently do, but not always, by any means. As they are willing to take quite small fish, even if they are themselves large specimens, there is a strong case for using small dead fish for bait. These are more likely to be taken fully into the mouth of the zander, so making secure hooking more certain. Probably a gudgeon is as good a bait as one could find.

Other fish

Under this heading comes a variety of different fishes about which there is little that one can say.

Char eat much the same food as trout but, except at or near spawning time, they are found at great depths, so that conventional fly fishing is impossible. *Powan* and other similar species are confined to relatively few lakes; they move about in large shoals which sometimes appear at the surface, causing a very obvious disturbance which local people at Loch Lomond, where this species is found, call 'finning'. The fish feed on creatures similar to those eaten by trout: small insects and

112

crustacea, and I have no doubt that they could be caught by fly fishing, using imitations of ephemerid nymphs, midge pupae and the like. The difficulty is location. I have often come across shoals of powan at the surface on Loch Lomond, when I have had no fly-fishing tackle with me. I have often gone out with fly-fishing tackle in the hope of finding powan, but have never succeeded. I have no doubt that an angler determined to catch powan on rod and line, who continued to go out after them day after day, and who sought information from local anglers on their whereabouts, would eventually succeed and, as his knowledge increased, succeed more and more frequently.

Gudgeon will eat almost anything they can get into their mouths, at any time of day or night. Their appetites can be stimulated by stirring up the bottom of a river with a rake or failing that, the end of a pole, or by wading and shuffling one's feet. They will feed with equal willingness in sunshine, dull weather or darkness and the water has to be very warm or very cold to put them off.

Ruffe are even more catholic in their feeding behaviour, though they are less willing to eat vegetable matter. In fact they look and behave very much like small perch, and there is really nothing more to say about them. Like gudgeon, they feed mostly at the bottom.

Bleak are entirely opposite, being for the most part surface feeders, but just as willing to eat anything they can swallow. *Bullheads* seem to eat only animal matter, at the bottom. They feed mostly after dark. *Minnows* on the other hand, while equally omnivorous, prefer to feed in daylight. *Spiny loach* live in tunnels in dense silkweed and eat what they can find there, including the silkweed itself. *Stone loach* live in gravel shallows.

The main importance of bleak, bullheads, gudgeon, minnows and loach to the angler is that they are eaten by a variety of other fish and can be used as baits. Dead minnows and loach, especially, appeal to barbel in June, and to chub, perch, trout, pike and zander at any time.

113

Flounders are found in the fresh water of some rivers, well above the salt estuary, and may also be found in some lochs. They seem to feed on any kind of animal matter, but the angler who wishes to catch them need look no farther than worms for bait. *Shad* run up some rivers to spawn, including the Wye and the Severn. Small bright spinners or fairly large gaudy flies catch them readily.

Part Three:

The Conditions

30 You can catch fish in hot weather

I have often said that it seldom pays to expend lots of effort in trying to catch fish, and especially big fish, during the middle hours of a hot summer's day. Generally speaking, that is true. There are exceptions, however, and there are also the times when, for one reason or another (usually trains, jobs or wives), these hours are the only ones available. So let's see what can be done to make the best of them.

As always in angling the first thing to do is find the fish. When the water is warm, the fish have more difficulty in finding oxygen, so they will naturally be in places where most oxygen is. In rivers this will be near fast water or waterfalls of any kind; in slack water that has been shaded all day, it will be perhaps by trees, and near weeds, which give off oxygen when they receive sunshine.

In lakes, again the weeds and well-shaded spots will be likely places. When there is a wind fish may be found where it is causing most ripple. If the lake is a very deep one, you may find that instead of seeking oxygen near the surface, the fish have gone down to where the water is cooler.

Apart from this last instance, hot weather has the general effect of bringing fish nearer the surface, and in summer at midday the light is bright and the water is usually clear. This means that unless you keep low, you are very likely to be seen by the fish, and so are other people. So it pays to try and find water that hasn't been disturbed by other people, and then take care not to disturb it yourself. If you make a careful search of undisturbed water you will very likely find shoals of fish basking at the surface. The chances of catching some of these fish are dependent on what species they are.

Chub, rudd, dace and roach all offer a good chance. Carp and bream are also found basking very often, but the chances of catching them then are fairly small. It takes hotter water to make tench bask, and I have never succeeded in catching one at such times. Perch and pike do bask on occasion and are sometimes willing to bite.

The first four fish I mentioned can all be caught by fly fishing when they are at the top, and you can choose wet or dry fly with an equal chance of success.

Whichever you choose, make sure the leader is sunk, whether the fly itself is floating or not — because if the nylon floats, it will make a great black shadow on the bottom like a writhing python and scare your fish for sure. Actually, that point applies however you decide to fish. In bright sunshine, sink the part of your line near the fish, otherwise you will cast that frightening shadow on the bottom or even across the fish themselves.

You need not necessarily use conventional fly-fishing tackle. You can put on an ordinary float, with an equal number of shot above and below it, close to it, or on the line alongside the float between the cap and the bottom ring. It doesn't have to be an artificial fly, either. Almost any real insect you can catch will do, and do very well.

Another very productive method is to tie a pear-lead (a stone will do in a pinch) to a long piece of finer nylon than that on your reel, and tie the free end of this fine nylon to your tackle about six inches above the hook. You don't need a float or any other lead.

What you have, in fact, is a simple paternoster with a weak link to its weight. That weak link is of such a length that it will reach from some suitable point on the opposite bank — or from some other convenient point, such as lily pads or rushes — to where the fish you are after are lying.

Now, you bait your hook with a live insect, or failing that, an artificial fly. You cast carefully and accurately so that your lead or stone lands where you intend it and stays there. Most times that will be on the opposite bank. But check your line as the weight lands, so that your line and fly remain in the air. Don't let them fall on the water.

118

Now, keeping your rod point high, move it until the fly is hanging over the nose of the fish you want to catch, and then let it 'dibble' up and down, only just touching the water.

If you hook the fish, and the weight sticks, either when you strike or at any time in playing the fish, the fine link will break leaving the fish still with you. Remember that the distance between hook and weight you need is usually about twice what you would guess, looking across a stream or pond.

Chub and big rudd will often take a cube of crust or a bunch of maggots, even in the hottest weather, if you can only get it to them without scaring them. And the less there is on the tackle apart from hook and bait, the less is the chance of scaring them.

If you do much of this sort of fishing, you will find that there is a lot more to it than choosing very fine tackle. Even the finest nylon you can buy will scare fish if you let it float, whereas quite stout nylon can remain unseen if it is just under the surface and runs away from the bait on the side opposite to the fish. So, when you use ordinary baits like crust and maggots and cheese in these conditions, remember that much more important than the bait or the tackle strength is finding the right way to use both. It pays handsomely to think twice before casting once, because you're not likely to be given a second chance with the same fish if you bungle your first attempt.

There are many other ways in which a few fish can be taken during these difficult periods, and they can sometimes catch you a splendid specimen. They are nearly always unorthodox ways, often ones that you think out on the spot. Now and then you can take advantage of some special happening, like caterpillars falling off overhanging trees, or by cattle stirring up mud, or by the opening of a sluice-gate.

There are such methods as using silkweed as bait in the rush of a weir-pool or letting a grasshopper or beetle down to where chub lie among the bushes. The midday angler has to be an opportunist, and a good-tempered one, too.

119

For of all forms of angling, this can be the most exasperating. Not only are you up against many purely angling difficulties — you are handicapped by your fellow-humans, not only non-anglers but anglers too. When you have spotted a big chub, made ready your tackle and spent twenty minutes crawling into position, getting stung by nettles, pricked by thistles and half-eaten by flies, so that when you arrive at the desired spot you're sweating like a bull, you're half-dizzy and know a first-class headache is well under way.

You've knelt on your sun-glasses and dropped your return-ticket in the grass never to be seen again. Then, just as you bait your hook with the grasshopper you've just caught with great labour, having lost the one you caught before you began the crawl, there will arrive at a brisk walk, a lover and his lass, clad in garments of vivid hue.

They will walk, hand in hand, to the water's edge; and the young man will say to you: 'Look, there's a fish! . . . Oh, it's gone now!' And of course, you'll reply: 'Was there really? Fancy my not seeing it!'

And smile all over your sweaty face.

31 Heat-wave effects on fish

It often happens, in hot weather like we have in some summers, that anglers catch big fish which, after the first rush, put up a disappointing fight. Even in an ordinary summer, fish seldom fight as long as they would have done had the water been cooler. I think this is probably due to the fact that the warmer and stiller the water is, the less oxygen it can hold. In such conditions, when a fish is using a lot of energy it suffers from the lack of oxygen. Naturally enough, species of fish that need a lot of oxygen are affected more than those that need little; so we find that such fish as pike and chub are apt to give up easily after one or two powerful rushes, whereas tench and carp often fight very hard. Of course, in fast-moving rivers there is more oxygen and consequently the fish are tougher and harder to land.

I have often noticed quite a difference in the staying powers of chub; for example, those caught in the lower reaches of the Ouse in warm weather, cannot keep up the struggle nearly as long as those of the upper river, where the water is not only faster moving but cooler because it is nearer the springs.

Another thing that I think affects the fighting powers of fish, especially big fish, is the amount they've eaten — no creature is as formidable on a full stomach as on a relatively empty one. A fish that has fed heartily all night has quite a load to carry around, which will make a difference to the fight it can put up if you hook it.

As I write, the rain is coming down very heavily, which reminds me that when the water is thick from rain, one's chances of landing a big fish on light tackle are very much better. A fish will not often dash off at high speed in thick water, simply because it can't see very well where it is going, and doesn't want to bang its nose against the bank, or a stone or boulder.

It is a fish's speed rather than its weight that smashes tackle and that isn't an opinion, it's a mathematical law. The pull created by a fish is proportional to its weight multiplied by the square of its speed. If a fish could double its *weight*, but go no faster, the pull needed to stop it would simply be *doubled*; whereas if its *weight* stayed the same while its *speed* were doubled, then the stopping pull needed would be *four times as great*. Thus, conditions that prevent a fish going at full speed give the angler a great advantage.

Probably the realisation that speed causes breakage is one of the reasons why masters of the art of playing fish, like Pete Thomas, are so successful. It is possible so to apply pressure to a hooked fish that it doesn't dash off. Big trout are beaten easily by this sort of playing technique, which was explained many years ago by G. E. M. Skues.

If you stand up in full view of a big trout you've hooked, and pull as hard as your tackle can stand, the fish will jump, rush and generally fight very strongly; but if you do your best to keep out of sight, that fish will cruise about in a bewildered sort of way until it is tired, especially if you keep the pull on it relatively light, and with a light pull, it is far less likely to go to weed.

But don't expect a chub to stay out of weed if you keep a light pressure on it. A chub will bolt into weed at the least sign of trouble, and only very firm handling will keep it out. If it does get in, in spite of all you can do to stop it, slack-off the line, wait a few minutes and then pull as hard and suddenly as the tackle lets you. That will fetch out the fish as often as not.

Whatever fish you are after, remember that you can lose big ones on the point of putting the net under them, if your net is bright and flashy or if you put it in with a splash. I like to have the net under water and held still long before my fish is brought near it.

32 Get into the weeds!

I still see hundreds and hundreds of anglers fishing in rivers during the middle hours of the day, in places where there are very few fish except tiddlers. In high summer, unless there has been recent rain and thus more current than usual, you won't find many good fish in the more open parts of the river. The warmer the water, the less the flow, and the brighter the sunshine, the more likely the good fish are to be in the narrow runs among the weeds.

The reasons are that the weeds produce oxygen when there is enough light, and the fish find food and cover amongst them. When the light decreases, the weeds stop producing oxygen, and begin to give off only carbon dioxide, which fish cannot breathe. Therefore, in the late evening, through the night, and in the early morning, fish will be in the open, weedless swims.

Very often you will hear an angler say: 'The fish were right off until 8pm; then they came on feed.' In fact, the probable reason why he caught nothing until about 8.30 was not because the fish were off feed, but rather that the fish weren't in his swim until then.

Not everyone can be fishing early and late. The angler who wants fish in the middle hours of a summer's day must learn to catch them where they are — among those weeds.

There are a few tricks worth knowing for fishing in such areas. First, if you're going to extract a big fish from weed, you need stronger tackle than you would use in an open swim. It will be more obvious to the fish, but you can reduce its scary effect somewhat by staining the nylon green or brown, to match the kind of weed where you are fishing. It pays also to use a green-bodied float (if you have to use a float at all). In fast runs, where quite a bit of lead is needed, it is better to use a small barleycorn lead than a number of big shot. For light loadings, you catch less weed with several little shots than with one big one.

Your float — where you use one — is less likely to catch up if it is attached by a bit of valve rubber at its extreme ends. Baits that cover the hook-point catch more fish and less weeds in these conditions, provided, of course, they don't pad the hook and hinder its ability to stick into the fish's mouth.

Now, what decides whether you use a float or not? It depends partly on what sort of fish you are after. You need no float to tell you when a chub bites, for example. Thus, I seldom use a float when fishing for chub or perch among the weeds, because a big bait (heavy enough to be cast easily) can be used, and these fish give a solid bite and hang on to the bait.

In some conditions, and on some rivers, you can catch roach and dace on floatless tackle; where they bite boldly and no long casting is needed, it pays to do without a float and feel for the bites. But where they bite shyly, or where a small bait is needed, then you have to use a float.

Fishing a run between weeds is much easier if you can get your rod-point over the run, or dead in line with the run from some position upstream. For roach and dace in these narrow runs, a long rod is a big help, and this is one of those cases where the carbon-fibre type, 12 to 14ft long, has its uses.

With chub, however, all you can do when you hook a fish is haul and hope, and then you need a more solid rod. Long rods are not too good for hauling tactics. If a chub gets weeded solid, don't pull, or hand-line it. Slack-off at once and wait for the fish to move away. It's an even chance he will, and when he does you can tighten up again. This doesn't seem to work so well with other fish, but it often succeeds with chub.

Don't use a lot of groundbait in narrow weed runs. All you need is two or three bits of hook-bait at intervals. If the run is very open and you cannot fish it without showing yourself, go upstream and stir up the bottom, so that the water runs muddy, move into position while it is still muddy, and then move as little as possible when it clears.

Those are some of the things to try when you are fishing

among weeds. There are many more ideas you yourself will think up to try. But there's nothing you can devise that will help you catch fish where there aren't any — in open, slack swims in the bright part of the day.

33 Watch those ditches when it rains

At the time of writing, the heavy rain that usually comes in September or November hasn't materialised, but it is bound to come, and when it does come, it sets some angling problems.

The effect it has on fishing varies enormously between one water and another. Rivers that flow through rich agricultural land are fed by hundreds of ditches as well as by springs and simple run-off, and nowadays, even those rivers that rise from the chalk take in a lot of water from ditches.

All through the summer, these ditches have been accumulating quantities of rubbish, mostly decaying vegetable matter, but in many cases there is other stuff as well, including artificial and natural manure, pest sprays, oil, road washings and sheep dip. As soon as there is enough water on the land, all this muck is washed into the river and the fish are often put off.

You should not be surprised, therefore, if the first flush of water produced by the autumn rains spoils your fishing. Don't make the mistake of judging subsequent rises in the flow of the river by the effect the first one had. *Once those filthy ditches have been washed reasonably clean, the fish will hang around at their mouths.*

There are exceptions, of course. Some ditches never seem to run clean; I've got one at the very top of my stretch of the upper Ouse. In certain conditions of heavy rainfall it pours in a horrible yellow torrent and when that is running in the fishing right down the stretch is always poor. This ditch evidently comes from or through a patch of soil that washes away easily and, while it isn't poisonous, it probably has a choking effect on the fish, rather as thick smoke would on humans. Fortunately, this stuff doesn't always afflict us even when we have high water. I don't know why it does sometimes but not on other occasions, but that's how it goes. We always go up and have a look if we think it may be playing its tricks.

Take a leaf out of our book, therefore, and check up on what is coming

126

out of ditch-mouths, feeder streams and land drains. If it looks nice and clean, fish near these places because they are probably bringing in worms, insects, and possibly warmer water. Often after a night frost you can catch good fish by the outfall of a land drain but nowhere else. But if the ditches or drains are pouring in filth, try and fish where the effect is least.

Another thing to watch are eddies. No doubt you know places on your river where nice big eddies form when the river is running high. I don't mean silly little whirlpools, but the eddies that form in bays, cow-drinks and at sharp bends, that let float tackle go round and round in a circle of from five to twenty yards in diameter. *What you must figure out is what is happening at the bottom.* Is the higher water stirring up all the accumulated mud, leaves, dead rushes and general rubbish that have been piling up all summer? Or has the river risen high enough to set an eddy over a nice bit of clean gravel, like you see at a cow-drink? If you cannot see, your plummet can help tell you.

Perhaps the eddy is depositing rubbish instead of washing it out. If it's a really big eddy, that may not be a drawback. The rubbish settles in the centre, so don't fish there; let your tackle go round and round it, or cast your leger to one side of the slack middle, into moving water.

Remember also the position of bulrush-beds. Now let's make this plain: I mean bulrush-beds, not reeds. Bulrushes are dark green when growing, have round stems and grow in sand or gravel. Reeds, of various kinds, and other species of rush, have round stems like baby bamboos and grow in mud. *Bulrush-beds in the current act as combs and breakwaters, even when they're reduced to brown stumps.* In high water, fish shelter in the areas just downstreams of these bulrush-beds. So fish there, but don't expect very definite bites, especially if the water is a bit cold. Fish will take baits and just stay put, so hit the least tremble or twitch.

On a river you can fish often, it pays to do some weed clearing in autumn. I know it sounds crazy, but if you cut away decaying lily plants or rushes, it will give later floods a better chance of washing the place clean, not only for the winter fishing but for next summer, too. In rivers where lily pads grow, the bottom can be pretty snaggy and lose you tackle, even in winter, unless you cut in the late autumn. These places are a sure roach-hold all through the winter and an hour's work will greatly improve their yield of fish for months ahead.

Many of the guests who fish our waters in winter are puzzled because some apparently clear swims cost them hook after hook while others fish easily. The answer is simple: the cutters have been through some swims but not others. *As long as it isn't going to upset other anglers, never hesitate to put a cutter through a winter swim. The fish will be back quite soon after the cutters have been packed away.* Places that hold lilies in summer almost always harbour fish in time of high water, and those that have been cleaned can give you splendid sport that you could never have had fishing a foul bottom.

Finally, when the water rises, change your tackle and baits. The swim that in August yielded fine roach to a single maggot on a No 16 hook, 1½lb line, with one BB shot and a little quill float, will in autumn probably need a 5lb line, a No 8, a small red worm or the tail of a lob, with either a swivelled leger lead or half-a-dozen strung swan shot; or if float fishing is possible, you will need a big float and plenty of lead.

I know it looks impossibly clumsy and most unlikely to succeed, but the longer you take to realise that high water demands drastic changes in how you fish, the more chances you'll be missing.

34 Work out the reactions of the fish

With modern drainage methods, heavy falls of rain are run off the land as quickly as possible, and where in the old days many of our rivers rose slowly and ran off slowly, we now find them coming up quickly and dirty.

Added to this on some rivers is the change in the methods of mill operation. When water mills were in use, their operators made full use of the water coming down the river. When there was too much, they drew just enough of their sluice-gates to let the surplus off. Nowadays, people who operate sluices seem to pull the lot at the first sign of a shower of rain.

However, all this does do something to counter the ill-effects of water abstraction. Water is being taken from the upper reaches of most of our rivers, and even from the springs, for domestic supplies. Less water going down the river means a reduced current and therefore more silting up. Some streams have been completely ruined in this way; anyone wanting to see actual cases can look at the Mimram and the Oughton in Hertfordshire.

In other instances, however, the extra water we get in the winter is run quickly into the river and rapidly down it through wide-open sluices, and the accumulated silt of the summer and autumn is shifted completely in the course of two or three of these semi-artificial spates.

From the long-term point of view that is a very good thing, but the back-end angler can expect little sport on a day when he finds the river coming down fast and full of muck. All this silt is very unlike the good, honest mud that is washed into a river by a summer cloudburst. It is a mixture of black, stinking silt and decaying vegetable matter, plus a whole lot of other stuff from all sorts of sources. It is not to be wondered at that the fish are put off feed, and the few you do catch look as if they have been through a bleaching bath.

That said, an angler living at or near the waterside and able to choose his day to fish can do very well when a spate comes. First of all, the fish move into sheltered spots as the water begins to rise, and are usually willing to feed. But they go off as the water thickens, and do not feed much again until the colour of the water clears. However, contrary to what most people think, it does that long before it has gone back to its normal level, and fish can be caught (if they can be found) almost directly the level begins to fall or the current slackens.

That isn't always the same thing, because sometimes somebody decides to wholly or partly close a sluice-gate, and then there is a considerable slow-down of current above the gate accompanied by a rise in level. Conversely, when gates are opened, there is often a fall in height accompanied by a faster current, having a disastrous effect upon the immediate prospects of catching fish because practically no slacks are left in which the fish can find shelter.

Where a good deal of river is available to the angler, it is sometimes possible to catch fish when the main river is running very thick, by finding a tributary that is still running clear (or relatively so). Fish will often move into such places, even when the current is strong, to get out of the filth in the main current.

The whole essence of finding fish under flood or semi-flood conditions is thinking out what their reactions will be. If you remember that they do not want to buck a strong current, but they would rather do that than stay in the thick mucky water, you will usually succeed in finding a spot that provides some sport. Don't expect too much, because by the time a fish has bucked a strong current and become half-suffocated by the muck it is carrying, it hasn't a tremendous amount of fight left in it.

Trotting-down float tackle in these circumstances is usually a waste of time. The method to adopt is legering or float legering, anchoring the bait really firmly with an ample allowance of lead. If the fish bite at all, they will bite strongly enough to move a horseshoe as a rule, but they won't grab at a bait that is dashing past, even if they see it (which is doubtful). So fix that bait firmly on the bottom and let the fish find it.

In most cases of this sort, you can fall back on one plan whenever you can't think of anything else, and that is choosing the slack side of the current and stret-pegging or tight-corking — or whatever you call it in your district — close to the bank and right under your rod-point. Even on a straight bit of river, the current is always slacker on one side than on the other; look for the side that has the most beds of rushes, and fish over the edge of the rushes, unless the beds are too wide. A long rod of 14 or 15ft is useful, and a roach pole enthusiast really comes into his element. If you do decide to fish over a rush-bed, be careful to avoid getting stuck in the mud!

35 So be a winter fisherman

I cannot understand why so many anglers practically give up fishing when autumn ends and don't begin again until the middle of June. I suppose the traditional ideas about the seasons are responsible. People visualise winter as a season of icy winds, snow and rain, and summer as a time of warmth and sunshine. But almost every year a lot more rain falls in summer than in winter, and even in the worst of winters, the days when it snows are few and far between.

When properly equipped, you can be just as comfortable and warm fishing in winter as you can in summer, and also more likely than at any other time to have good sport with some kinds of fish. The secret is knowing what to fish for on any given day, and a thermometer will help to tell you that.

Chub, perch and pike go on feeding until the water temperature drops below about 35°F (2°C), while grayling will still feed in even colder water. Roach and dace go off feed if the water gets much below 40°F (4°C), and bream won't stand it much colder than about 45°F (7°C). Of course, these aren't hard-and-fast rules and you are sure to find exceptions, but generally speaking they are true and if you fish accordingly, you'll avoid a lot of wasted time.

If you arrive to find water temperature above 45°F (7°C), and the weather is such that you think it will stay over 45°F until dusk, you can please yourself what you fish for. Roach, rudd, dace, bream, chub, perch, pike and grayling are all likely to feed during some part of the day at least. But if the temperature is, say, 43°F (6°C) and doesn't seem likely to rise, you had better forget about bream and rudd. If it's under 40°F (4°C) you won't catch many roach or dace either, and if you want sport you will be well advised to go after chub or grayling, perch or pike. Of course you must watch out for changes and keep on trying the temperature, in case later in the day you miss chances of catching fish that rising temperature has brought on feed.

Still waters in winter fish very differently from rivers, and if you find the temperature at the surface is below 39°F (4°C), the bottom will be the warmest place. If, however, you find it is over about 40°F (4°C) at the top, it will be warmer there and you may get good roach, pike and perch in quite shallow water.

In rivers the temperature doesn't vary much between surface and bottom because the current keeps the water well mixed, and here you have to locate your fish by watching the current, as in winter they will be in fairly deep water for most of the time.

We all know about lay-bys and slacks, and how they are supposed to be the best places to fish in winter, especially when there's a lot of water coming down the river. But just casting into slack water isn't good enough: in nine cases out of ten, there's one place and one alone where you will find fish in lay-bys and slacks, and that is at the edge of the main current. If you can fish from the upstream edge of the slack, cast into the main current and let it roll your bait into the slack; you should get fish if they are there and willing to feed. You must search all along the edge of that current, letting your float or light leger go down the current a little further each cast before you stop more line going out and let the bait swing in, dragging bottom all the time.

This kind of fishing is no place for small hooks and baits, nor for very fine tackle. If you're after chub or big bream, a knob of paste, with or without cheese, as big as a walnut, or else a full-sized lob, on No 8 or No 6 hooks, are about right, and even for roach and dace a lobworm tail or a paste ball as big as a marble are not too big fished on a No 12 or No 10 hook. You may get one or two nice roach in a netful of small stuff by fishing maggots or wheat, or other small baits, but if you are after specimens offer them a good mouthful.

Winter fishing, as a rule, means fairly short-range work in running water, though like everything else in fishing there are plenty of exceptions. But close-in fishing gets results on most occasions and this is particularly true when it's pike or perch you are after. Fishing at this time poses many problems you don't meet in summer, but it brings many advantages: fewer weeds, fewer boats, a cleaner bottom, and hungrier, harder-fighting fish, with the chances of a glass-case specimen, or even a record breaker, greatly increased with several kinds of fish.

The angler who fishes only in summer and autumn is only half an angler.

36 Even when it's cold these fish will be feeding if . . .

When we have to face colder conditions, it is well to consider which species will be most profitable to pursue.

Carp, tench and barbel are unlikely to oblige during the last five months of the season, except under special conditions, but before dismissing these species we ought to think about what those conditions are, so that if they do occur, we can perhaps take advantage of them.

I think they occur when either there is an exceptional rise in water temperature, or when the fish have been forced to take a lot of exercise. Where carp and tench are found in rivers, they become torpid as temperature falls in the autumn and seek quiet places where they lie inert on the bottom, perhaps partly buried in mud. In rivers where such places are available to them, like the Thames and the Kennet, barbel do the same. They move out of the fast runs and go into deep holes and slacks where there is next to no current.

Under such conditions, the fish use no energy, and the low temperature slows down what is known as their metabolic rate, that is, their rate of living and growing. So they do not feed.

But suppose the river rises and the current speeds up through these slack places. The fish then have to swim against it or else be washed pell-mell down the river. They may move to the slowest current they can find, but they will have to use quite a lot of energy whatever they do, and that energy they must replace by feeding. If it isn't replaced, they will be weakened more and more by successive spates until they lack the strength to buck the current. From an angling point of view, then, we can expect chances of catching barbel, tench, or carp in water temperatures far below those at which they would normally feed whenever these fish have been forced to do a good deal of swimming.

That probably explains why barbel in the Hampshire Avon are often caught at intervals throughout the winter; the Avon is fast, and places where barbel can lie-up out of the current are few and far between, whereas in the slower Thames and Kennet they are seldom taken after the end of October.

Tench and carp are not often caught in winter from ponds and lakes, but rivers continue to yield them whenever heavy water has stirred them up. The same thing applies to bream, though to a lesser extent, because bream will feed at lower temperatures, anyway. I have always found them willing to feed at some time of day if the flow is normal and the temperature above 50°F (10°C), but below 45°F (7°C) they seldom feed unless the flow of the river has been considerably increased. Let the river come down thick and heavy, and even with water temperature as low as 40°F (4°C) you have a good chance of catching bream if you can find them.

There, of course, is the snag. A friend of mine was once talking to that well-known Thames professional fisherman, the late John L. Webb, and told me that Mr Webb had expressed his opinion in no uncertain terms about certain river reports that had said the Thames needed a good flush.

'The Thames is a big river,' said Mr Webb, 'and the fish are hard enough to find as it is without any flushes to shift them about so they have to be found all over again!'

With fish like roach, dace, chub and perch a flush, especially on one of the bigger rivers, can be a curse. Thick water sickens and puts off these fish anyway, and on top of that it moves them to different places. Sometimes a really heavy flood alters the river-bed and affects the position of the fish permanently. But with other species, a flush may at least stir up fish that otherwise would not have fed at all, even though it also may move them to different places.

Then is the time to study the set of the currents, relate them to your knowledge of the river, its depths and contours, and think out where the fish are most likely to be. It is no time for visiting strange waters, but it may be a golden opportunity to come to grips with specimen fish in rivers you know well. Find them away from their usual haunts and snags, in water free from weed and willing to take a bait, and you have a splendid chance of bringing some of them to net.

Finding them, the first essential in catching any fish at any time, is up to you.

37 How do you catch fish on those freezing winter days?

When the water temperature falls below the critical temperature of 39.2°F (4°C), there is a drastic change in the behaviour of fresh-water fish. The faster the temperature falls, and the lower it goes, the greater the effect, but in any case the figure of 39.2°F is critical.

Immediately after the temperature has fallen below it, fish eat a great deal less, and in rivers they tend to move out of the main current and into the slow or slack water. In big lakes, they move into deeper water as the temperature falls, and if a lake is deep enough, find areas where the temperature never gets below about 42°F (6°C), all through the winter. In such waters, they can always avoid water below that critical 39.2°F (4°C) and if you are able to find them and get a bait to them you can catch them. In the shallower lakes and ponds, and in rivers, the fish can't avoid being in water below 39.2°F. After they have been in it for several days, they start feeding again, though never as freely as they do in warmer water.

I have been asked why fish won't feed at times, even on bright, sunny autumn and winter days when it is warm enough on the bank to cause anglers to take their coats off. Well, the answer is that a spell of sunny autumn and winter days is associated with clear nights, and clear nights mean high temperature loss by radiation. The fall in water temperature at night is not fully restored by the sunshine on the following day. You may be sitting there on the bank, enjoying the warmth of the sun, but stick a thermometer in the water, and it will show you that although you may feel warm, the fish do not!

Remember, however, that if you are fishing a deep lake, with areas of bottom below twenty feet or so, sunshine is very welcome. On a dull day there isn't much light below twenty feet, but if the sun shines the light level down there is much higher.

Now, just as some fish feed very little when the light is too bright, others don't feed much if it isn't bright enough. Perch are the chaps that like enough light; remember, you don't catch many after dusk in the summer, do you? All right, if you know a deep lake holding big perch, bless the autumn and winter sunshine that provides enough light in the deep holes to start them feeding. Pike, too, though to a lesser extent.

The fish that do not like too much light are affected just as much in autumn and winter as they are in summer. Roach, for example, may keep you waiting till the light begins to fail before they will bite freely, whether it is June or December. I have caught them after dark in winter, when there have been no bites in daylight.

What do you do if the water is below 39.2°F (4°C) and there are no areas of water that you can find where it is warmer? First, find slow or slack water. Second, rig tackle that will stay put where you cast it, but which can be moved to cover an area of bottom. Third, though this isn't an invariable rule, use smaller baits than usual. Fourth, use very little groundbait as the fish don't want too much food; nor do they feel inclined to dash about. Thus you must move your bait to them, but very slowly, so as to give them time to take it without their having to move quickly. And fifth, use sensitive tackle that lets you detect delicate bites, because delicate bites are what you will be most likely to get. You move your bait, a little at a time, letting it dwell between each move. Eventually, it comes close to the fish, so that he can suck it in. He does, but he isn't going anywhere; he is sluggish. You're not going to see much of a bite-indication, are you? That is why you need sensitive tackle.

Water colour has two effects. It deludes anglers into thinking the fish can't see them, so they stand bolt upright, getting between water and sky. The fish are scared, because no matter how little light reaches them, if there is any at all it will be reduced once an angler gets between the fish and the sky. They cannot actually see you, but they know you are there. Imagine you are in a room that has frosted-glass windows; if someone passes a window, you know it, don't you? Right, fish know if you pass their window, so don't do it. Water is never as coloured as it looks. It might appear to be little better than mud, but dip out a jam-jar full and you will be surprised by how clear it is.

The other effect of coloured water is to reduce light penetration. That may cause such fish as roach to feed in brighter general light conditions than they would feed in if the water were clearer. It may also prevent perch or pike from feeding because it cuts out too much light.

Coloured water affects different rivers in different ways. Provided the temperature isn't too low, some colour in rivers that are mainly rain-fed, and that includes the Thames and the Ouse, will often cause fish to feed quite keenly. The same amount of colour in a spring-fed river, such as the Hampshire Avon or the Test, will put fish right off. It takes a good deal of practical fishing experience to enable an angler to judge the effects of colour in the rivers he fishes.

Colour in the water puts a premium on worms for bait, which is logical after all. The colour is usually caused by an increasing current, or a rise in the water, washing soil and worms from the banks.

One effect of very cold water that is often overlooked is its effect on baits. Worms will wriggle in water so cold that maggots are rigid, and pastes become considerably stiffer, especially cheese paste; so if you expect to fish in very cold water, mix your paste much softer. There is a case for using casters instead of maggots, but the advantage of maggots, even without wriggle, is that you can see if you have had a bite without any indication, because your maggot comes up with its inside missing. Then you know you are fishing in the right place.

38 It's the current that counts

Currents can be very deceptive, especially at a time of year when more and more water is coming down our rivers. You can be fishing in one place and groundbaiting in another if you aren't careful. I got caught like that not long ago.

There's a nice-looking swim on a river I often fish. The current is concentrated along the left bank for some distance, and then sweeps diagonally across to the other side, being deflected by a shelving bank of gravel. You can sit and fish with the current going straight away from you. Drop in a float almost at your feet and it runs steadily away, right across the river. There's a clean gravel bottom all the way. A nice bed of bulrushes on the upstream side of the crossover current, and a high, overhanging bank on the far side, make it a very attractive-looking place to fish, and the obvious method seemed to be to trot a float down the current with the bait just tripping the bottom. All that seemed necessary to get the groundbait in the right place was to drop it in at one's feet.

I fished it like that several times, and so did others. We caught nothing. The other day I came to this swim at about 3pm, groundbaited as usual and began trotting down float tackle. Now, I should explain that to work the tackle over the bank of gravel that caused the current to cross the river, I had to hold the float well back to let the hook and shot swing up somewhat, because the depth was set for the water the other side of the gravel bank.

It suddenly occurred to me that although the surface water was going over this bank — taking my float tackle with it — the water near the bottom would be deflected across the river much more than that at the top, and it would be the course of the water near the bottom that would carry my groundbait.

So I stopped fishing and tried to work out where my

groundbait would be. Well to the right of the surface current, I thought, and probably settled on the bottom somewhere in that direction. I increased the distance between float and shot, added a couple more shot and commenced laying-on, with a bit of cheese paste the size of a pea for bait.

After searching a bit, I got a good knock and caught a 4oz dace; then a small roach; then a ½lb dace, a 6oz dace, and a chub of 1¼lb. After the commotion of landing the chub — even a small one can nip round pretty smartly on light tackle — there was a wait of ten minutes or so before the next fish. This was a roach well over a pound. By this time it was nearly dark, so I packed up. I hadn't caught anything spectacular, but I felt very pleased at having found out about that swim.

There are lots of swims in which the surface current can lead you badly astray, especially if you float-fish, because float tackle will always follow the surface current, while the water deeper down may be going another way. If you have any reason to suspect this, there are several ways of tackling the problem.

One is to use very heavy, solid groundbait and to throw it in good big lumps, adding stones if necessary. Such groundbait will stay where it is thrown, and you can be sure you are fishing near it. Alternatively, if you put in loose groundbait, you will either have to search to find where it has attracted the fish, or, if the swim is suitable, use a floatless tackle, lightly weighted, and let the current take charge of it.

It is often surprising where such tackle has got to when you pull it up again. Of course, even with floatless tackle, the surface current may take charge of your line if the loading is wrong, or if you cannot steer things with your rod so that the bait follows the current at the bottom.

There are all sorts of different situations to contend with, and the important thing is to use your head and think about the swim you are fishing. Try and visualise what the water at the bottom (where the fish are) is doing. It is the current that matters more than ever at those times of year when the water is coloured and your bait must find the fish.

39 Put your bait where the fish are

Finding where the fish are and putting your bait, fly or other lure where they can take it, without scaring them, are the most important factors in successful angling. Here I want to talk about the business of placing your bait.

First, casting accuracy. You are not as accurate as you think you are! The reason for that is that the farther you cast, the smaller your error appears to be. Some of the books about fishing talk complete nonsense about the standard of accuracy that anglers are supposed to achieve. The other day I read in a tackle catalogue of the 1920s that David Foster of the famous Ashbourne firm of tackle-makers, used to demonstrate his fly-casting skill by dropping his fly in a floating walnut shell! If you can drop a fly into a 30in ring, 15yd away, every time, you are brilliant. Join the British Casting Association and enter the trout-fly accuracy event. You'll win it.

As for casting plugs, legers and things of that sort, a good caster should hit a 30in ring at 20yd, twice out of three attempts, but only if he is prepared to cause a considerable splash — one that would scare the fish in the area.

So what can the average angler do to improve his accuracy? Let's take fly casting. Never cast farther than you need, because the farther you cast the worse your accuracy gets. And always aim at something at every throw, such as a bit of floating weed, a small calm patch in the ripple, a bit of foam or a bubble. Do this even when there are no fish rising, or when you are fishing deep, and just covering the water in the hope that a fish will see and take your fly. The same applies when you are float fishing, legering, free-lining, paternostering or spinning. Always select a point of aim and cast at it; that's the way to learn accurate casting.

Perfect accuracy being impossible, there are ways in which you can reduce the effect of error. For example, if you're fly fishing on a still water, and you think fish are at or near the surface, fish across the wind, if possible. That way, more fish will see your fly; they will see it in side view and if they take it, you will have a better chance of hooking them. If you cast a bit too far, ahead of a moving fish, the retrieve will pull the fly across his track.

With leger tackle, you can often compensate for error and at the same time avoid scaring fish by the splash of your lead if you cast well beyond the place where the fish are, and then either wind the bait back into position, or let the current take it there.

Suppose you wish to place your bait in a spot twenty yards away. Cast forty yards, if the area of water lets you, and wind back. Your bait can be up to about twelve feet off the proper line, and still be pulled back into the correct place, because you can lay your rod over to your left or to your right before you start pulling back. By fast reeling in, you can keep your bait, or your lead on the surface, and let it sink exactly where you want it to be. In a river with a good current you can often cast down and across and, with your rod-point high, let the current swing your tackle round, dropping the rod top when it is in the right place. This method can be used to place a leger, or to put float tackle in position to start trotting. It is much better than dropping the tackle directly to where you want it, especially when the conditions demand a heavy lead or heavily weighted float tackle.

There is another aspect of accuracy which gets less attention than it deserves and that is in respect of depth, especially in still-water fly fishing. If you find the trout are deep down, you won't get far, even with a sinking line, unless your fishing depth is under control. So use a watch with a second hand to check the sinking time you allow; if you keep varying the sinking time till you catch a fish, you will need to know which time allowance was successful and guesswork won't do.

Roughly, a slow-sinking line sinks a foot every seven seconds, a medium sinker a foot every five seconds and a high-density sinks a foot every three seconds. In other words, the fastest-sinking line, short of a lead core, needs an allowance of a full minute's sinking time to get down 20ft. If you think you can guess accurately when sixty seconds has elapsed without a watch with a second hand, try it!

You can estimate the depth of lakes by timing how long a lead of given weight and shape takes to sink. Time it in water of known depth, then you can calculate by proportion how deep any bit of water is, if you know the time the lead takes to sink in it. Very useful, when you are searching a lake to find the deepest holes, whose whereabouts you need to know if, for example, you are after big perch in winter.

On large still waters, finding accurate depths can make a tremendous difference to your catches, not only in winter but in summer. I'll tell you why.

One of the most important food items in such waters are tiny crustacea, of which the best known is daphnia. Many kinds of fish feed on them, and other kinds eat little fish that are feeding on daphnia. Now, the daphnia are very fussy about light intensity; they want it just right, so they change their depth to get it right. On a dark night they are just under the surface; on a bright sunny day, in clear water, they may be forty feet down. Where they are, so are most of the fish, most of the time.

Any photographer who has an exposure meter can measure light intensity at the surface, and if he relates this to the clarity of the water, he can with experience guess fairly accurately how deep fish will be, at any time of the day or night.

I cannot sufficiently over-stress the importance of accuracy in placing your bait or lure, in respect of direction, distance and, often, depth. It can make a tremendous difference to your catches in every branch of angling.

So very often we hear anglers say: 'The fish are off feed today!' Sometimes that is true; much more often what appears to be unwillingness on the part of fish to feed is really failure by the angler to put his bait where they are. Most anglers change bait, fly or lure if they aren't catching fish. They would do well to realise that nothing will succeed unless it is put where the fish are.

40 The lessons to be learned

Fishing a turbulent bit of current a few days ago, I saw my float dip; I struck and felt nothing. I hadn't expected to feel anything, because from the way the float had moved I thought it was probably only a bit of weed on which the hook had caught. But when I examined the two maggots on my hook, I found there was nothing left of them but the skins. I had had a real bite after all, and I knew pretty well what kind of fish was responsible.

Roach, rudd, bream and dace are the fish that treat maggots so, and as I knew there wouldn't be rudd or bream in that swim, it must have been a roach or dace that was responsible. Before I had that bite I didn't know whether or not the swim held any fish. It was a bad day for fishing, with bites few and far between. But after seeing those maggot skins I persevered and got a few nice roach. If I hadn't taken notice of the effect of different fish bites on maggots, and on other baits, I might have given up that swim and as likely as not moved to a worse one. Thus, examination of the bait can often teach you quite a lot about what fish are in a swim.

Sometimes you retrieve your maggots to find they have been perforated. That could be the work of a perch, or a small pike or chub. Missing a decisive bite and finding your maggots absolutely unmarked often means the bite came from minnow, gudgeon or other quite small fish, but it can also mean you missed a big tench or a chub. If you know the spot you are fishing well, you can usually guess what is responsible.

Worms, too, often give you a clue about what you missed. If your bait is a big lobworm, and you miss a good bite and find part of your worm is missing, it tells you very little. If the break in the worm is where the hook was stuck in, the bite might have been from a fish of any size, but if the break is somewhere else, the chances are that a fairly small fish was responsible. This is by no means an invariable rule, because sometimes a big fish will take hold of the end of a worm, so that when you strike the worm breaks. But if you keep missing bites and find the end of the worm is being taken off, you can usually attribute it to fairly small fish. If, however, you retrieve a big worm and find it full of small perforations, suspect some kind of fish with teeth, like a pike, trout, perch or chub. The most distinct holes in the worm are made by pike. With the other three fish, the worm is more mangled than perforated. Of course, a worm is sometimes cut about and chewed by crayfish, but you can generally tell if they are responsible from a combination of knowledge of the water you are fishing and the form a crayfish bite takes.

My inclusion of chub among fish with teeth may surprise some people, but in fact not only have all fish of the carp family got teeth, but chub, especially, have a set of mincing-machine cutters down their throats that are amazing effective.

A friend of mine who was doubtful about this once tried to find out for himself by shoving his finger down the throat of a four-pounder and as a result was unable to use that finger again for a fortnight. He was lucky to get it back at all.

The throat teeth of a chub that size can smash a whole, hard, full-sized crayfish to pulp, or they can cut a small fish in half as cleanly as you could do it with a sharp knife. If, when you're livebaiting with a minnow or gudgeon, or some other small fish, you see one sharp bob of the float, or a single smart twitch on the line, and nothing more, and then when you reel up find that the body of your fish has been neatly chopped off, leaving just the head on your hook, depend upon it a chub was responsible. There is no British fish with more devastating teeth than the chub. A pike's teeth are mere pins by comparison.

Another indication of the nature of a biter you didn't catch is sometimes seen on a live- or dead-fish bait. It consists of a more or less semi-circular piece nipped out from the belly of the bait, generally at or near the vent. That is the work of a good-sized eel, and it is usually possible to catch the culprit by using a smaller bait, dead, and lying on the bottom and giving the eel plenty of time when you get the next bite.

Evidence of having had a bite from any fish with throat teeth, and that includes roach, rudd, chub, bream, dace, carp, barbel, gudgeon, tench and minnows, shows as a rule that you ought to have hooked the fish responsible since it is unlikely that the biting fish could have got the bait as far down as its throat teeth without having the hook in its mouth.

It *can* happen when a small dace tries to swallow a big worm. One end may be chewed while most of the worm and the hook are still outside the mouth of the fish. But otherwise, a marked bait with fish of the carp family means a chance missed, and that, in turn, should cause you to think how you can alter your rig so that you get a more sensitive indication of a bite.

41 Once bitten, twice shy

If you catch a fish and return it, what are the chances of that fish being caught again? Will it have learnt from its experience?

Well, different species of fish behave differently and one of the biggest mistakes that anglers and scientists can make is to assume that what applies to one sort of fish must also apply to others. There is as much difference between a perch and a roach as there is between a cat and a rabbit. There is also reason for thinking that individual fish may behave differently from others of the same species, even in the same water.

Recently, some experiments carried out by Dr J. J. Beukama of Gronigen State University in Holland, were reported in *New Scientist* and elsewhere. Briefly, they showed that a carp caught on rod and line, and returned to the water, became much harder to catch. Even a year later such a fish remained, according to Dr Beukama, between three and four times as difficult to catch as were carp that had never been caught before.

I don't know the full details of the experiment; I wish I did. It would be interesting, for example, to know whether different baits were tried and how the carp reacted. That would give us some idea about whether the carp that had been caught associated their capture with a particular kind of food, or whether they had learnt to avoid any bait attached to a line, or both.

My experience leads me to think that carp are well able to learn to avoid a bait that is obviously attached to a line. I say 'obviously' because a drab-coloured line on the bottom is not nearly as noticeable as one floating on the surface. It would also be interesting to know if Dr Beukama's experiments showed any indication of whether carp can learn from one another.

There are some species of fish that seem to me to be far less able to learn from experience than others. I've known the same

149

tench to be caught three times in the same swim, on the same day. A barbel in the Royalty fishery was caught, if my memory serves me well, about nine times in ten days. I've caught the same pike twice in a day, more times than I can remember, but I cannot be sure whether that means that pike, barbel and tench are really less able to learn, because the fish that obviously haven't learnt may be exceptional individuals.

Certainly, tench react over a period. It's quite common to make big bags of tench early in the season on lobworms, and then to find that in July you catch few on lobworms but plenty on breadflake. Later still in the season, they go off breadflake and you get them on mussel, stewed wheat, tiny crust cubes or maggots. It does seem that they have learned something through being caught and returned.

About roach and dace I can't say much because most waters hold large numbers, and the individuals are difficult to identify. On heavily fished waters, though, it isn't at all uncommon to catch examples of both species with their top lips missing, and such fish must have had experience of the effects of fish-hooks!

I think chub are very good learners. That doesn't mean that a chub is never caught twice, but their reactions to baits that have caught them before are very noticeable. They don't want to know! I think it is the bait rather than the line or hook that they learn to fear, and I am quite sure that such fear is infectious. If one chub in a shoal makes off when he sees a bait that has caught him before, the others in the shoal usually refuse that bait, even if they don't bolt.

Roach can communicate, too. If one roach in a shoal samples a bait and spits it out, it is very rare for any other roach in that shoal to take it. If I catch a roach, I always change the bait even if it looks perfectly all right, because I have reason to think that any bait that has been in and out of a roach's mouth is unattractive to other roach. I can't prove it, and I may be wrong, but that is what I think.

I'm quite sure that perch learn by experience, and I think too that the bigger they are the better they are able to learn.

Odd fish, perch; sometimes they seem to show considerable intelligence, sometimes they act plain stupid. I don't know any other species that is so successful at making fools out of expert anglers!

I never set much store by the stories about kids coming along with bent pins and sticks and catching huge fish when all the experts are baffled. I have never known that to actually happen, though I've often caught a good fish when all the kids with bent pins and sticks were baffled. All the same, big perch do quite often come along and attach themselves to indifferent tackle used by anglers who are far from expert, in waters where better anglers, better equipped, have fished for them in vain.

About trout, I am in no doubt whatever. A trout needs only one lesson about the danger of an artificial fly, and having had it, he is frightened if he sees the same pattern again in the same place. I've been told that scientific experiments on trout have shown that it takes a good many experiences to condition the fish, to teach them anything. Well, it isn't true: one experience is enough. Dr Beukama has proved that one experience is enough to teach carp, and the same applies to trout. A trout can tell the difference between an artificial mayfly with grey wings and one with green wings. If he's been taught to avoid the green-winged one, through having been caught on it and put back, he'll bolt or take cover if he sees it again, at any rate for the next three or four weeks. But you can catch him on the grey-winged artificial — once! How long his memory lasts I do not know. Dr Beukama's carp remembered for at least a year, but I am inclined to think that trout have shorter memories.

Generally speaking, though, I think we know enough to say that practically all fish that are caught and returned become more difficult to catch again to some extent; that on heavily fished waters it therefore pays to change baits and that the more successful any bait, lure, plug, spinner or fly is when first tried, the sooner its effectiveness will deteriorate.

Fish can and do learn by experience, and to be successful you have got to stay one jump ahead of what they know.

42 How to tempt sleeping fish

I was listening to the radio programme 'The Living World' the other day, and heard the panel answering the question, 'Do fish sleep?' Fortunately they had a real authority on fish to give an opinion on this, in the person of Alwyne Wheeler of the Natural History Museum at South Kensington, and his answer was that fish do indeed sleep.

Unfortunately, and I am sure unintentionally, the panel then went on to give the impression that all fish go to sleep as soon as it is dark, and stay asleep until it gets light again. They quoted an experience of a former director of a zoo aquarium, who switched on the lights in the middle of the night and found all the fish lying inert on the bottom.

Of course, it is true that fish sleep. But how much their sleeping is related to the state of the light is hard to say. I have seen some sorts of fish, now and then, showing every appearance of sleeping in broad daylight, even in bright sunshine. Only a week ago I spotted two or three trout in the exceptionally clear water at Damerham, lying absolutely motionless on the weed at the bottom. They stayed that way until my leaded nymph touched one, whereupon it started forward, swam round in a circle, and stopped again in its former position.

Most anglers have seen carp lying perfectly still at the surface in sunshine. We say 'They're basking', but it seems quite likely that they are actually asleep. Tench occasionally behave in the same way, and so do roach and rudd.

It is difficult to tell when a fish is asleep. The fact that a shadow passing over apparently sleeping fish will scare them doesn't prove they are asleep. We are easily awakened by sound because even when we are asleep, our ears still work, though our eyes are closed. Fish cannot close their eyes, so it seems reasonable to assume that they can see in their sleep, and can wake quickly.

No doubt their sense of smell also operates in their sleep. Sometimes I come across one of my friends in the cat family sound asleep, and I put a little bit of blue cheese near its nose. After a minute the cat's whiskers start twitching, and then the animal wakes up, chomps the cheese, and goes back to sleep.

So it seems to me likely that if you drop a smelly bait near a sleeping fish, that fish may smell the bait in its sleep, wake up and take the bait, if it fancies it. And groundbait of the right sort may wake up a whole shoal of fish and start them feeding, at any time of the day or night.

We all know that some sorts of fish feed at night, while others start feeding in earnest only when the light begins to fail. Some years ago, Fred J. Taylor and I did some experiments on the upper Ouse and found that the big roach started feeding keenly as soon as a photographic exposure meter registered 6.5 foot-candles, reflected from the backs of our hands. There's no magic about that figure, which simply related to the depth and clarity of the swims we happened to be fishing. But the experiments did show that the amount of light reaching the fish was quite critical. It now seems likely that what was actually happening was that the angle of the sun dropped below 10°.

From then on, these roach would keep feeding till about 11 or 11.30pm and then stop. They would come on again about half an hour before first light and continue to feed until the light again reached 6.5 foot-candles, or, more likely, till the sun's angle got to about 10° again. It seems probable that the period in the night when they didn't bite was their sleeping time.

We have any amount of evidence that some kinds of fish stay awake even in the darkest night; bream, carp and eels are likely to bite at any time in the hours of darkness. But there are other species, like chub, barbel and tench, that normally cease to feed during the middle hours of darkness, and others that seem to do little feeding at all in the dark.

Pike, perch and dace are sometimes caught in the dark, but not very often, and I think that they probably sleep most of the

153

night away. Trout, on the other hand, are often active all through the night and I fancy they do most of their sleeping in the daytime.

Sometimes you see a pike lying absolutely motionless, and when you run a spinner or plug across the front of his nose, he takes no notice at all. Keep on working that spinner and very often you will eventually see him become alert, and at the next cast take the lure. Perhaps he was asleep when you first saw him, but the repeated passage of your spinner near him has awakened him.

You may start tench feeding by doing a bit of work in your swim with a weed-drag. We have always thought that this stirs up the mud and makes a lot of mud-dwelling creatures, such as bloodworms, available to the tench. But is that really what happens? You can be fishing in a tench swim that you've groundbaited, and getting no bites, though the groundbait is there waiting for the tench to eat it. Yet if you put the weed-drag through, you often start catching fish. Could it be simply that the disturbance which dragging causes wakes up sleeping tench?

Some ghillies on salmon rivers firmly believe that when salmon are proving impossible to tempt, it pays to hurl a succession of large stones into their lies. It sounds pretty drastic, but I am told it is often successful. If salmon are not only resting in a pool, but are actually asleep, they might well notice flies, Devons or prawns after being woken up by a few rocks.

As I said in Chapter 22, I once kept two very small perch in an aquarium. Often I'd see them lying on the bottom, not moving, but if I dropped a little water in which a few worms had been washed into their tank, their back fins would be raised and they would swim wildly round their tank, on the look-out for worms. That seems to me to show not only that fish can detect smells or flavours in the water, but that they can be awakened when they are sleeping.

One often hears anglers say, when they're not getting bites: 'Oh, all the fish are asleep!' They say it in jest, but often enough they may be absolutely right; the fish actually are asleep. A handful of the right groundbait may wake them up and start them feeding.

43 Conclusions

I hope that what I have written will be of some help to readers, but it cannot help unless one or two other things that affect the feeding of fish are remembered.

The thumping vibration of an angler's boots along the bank quite destroys the appetite of nearly all kinds of fish, and so does the shutting off of some of the light by a man getting between the fish and part of the sky. And no matter how much I'm able to tell you about what fish feed on when they aren't scared, you won't catch many on what they might have eaten if you hadn't scared them.

I have learnt from a good many years' experience of writing about fishing, that whenever I say something like that, someone will write telling how *he* caught fish while dressed in a white shirt and stamping for all he was worth, or something of that kind. And he's probably telling the truth, because fish are not 100 per cent predictable in their behaviour. Take no notice of him, however. Continue to find where the fish are, to avoid scaring them, and to choose the right tackle; you'll then find knowledge of their feeding habits very useful to you.

Except in the case of predatory fish, it is unusual to be able to use their natural food for bait, and knowing what they eat naturally is of most use in the clues it gives you about how and where fish get their food.

Although other baits have their uses at times, it is rare to find fish that can't be caught on bread, worms, maggots or small fish, and none of these are in the least bit improved by being doused with stuff from the chemist's shop. No essence or flavouring on earth can make a bait attractive to a fish that isn't there or which has been scared off. And a fish that is there and isn't scared will usually take a perfectly ordinary bait if you take care to offer it in the right way.

Bearing all that in mind, there are two basic ways in which

you can use knowledge of how conditions affect the feeding of the various kinds of fish. You either set out to fish for a particular species, using your knowledge to help you choose the best spot, the best time, the best tackle and the best tactics to suit the conditions you find when you arrive at the waterside, or else you wait until you've arrived and seen what the conditions are, and then decide which sort of fish is likeliest to provide sport under those conditions.

Suppose, for example, you are going to a river that holds big roach and good chub. If you're a roach specialist and determined to catch roach that day, and on arrival find it much too warm and bright for the big ones to bite, you'll spend the time until evening choosing a swim, plumbing the depth, perhaps trimming a few weeds, and generally getting everything well sorted out and ready for the time when you expect the roach to start feeding. But if you don't mind what kind of fish you catch, but want to get at some fish immediately, you'll fix chub tackle and put in a few hours stalking chub, casting into likely spots, and so on, perhaps changing to roaching later on when the chances seem better.

Sometimes you can combine several kinds of fishing in one day, going after each in turn at the time that suits it best. Do remember, though, that nobody can lay down the law about the behaviour of fish, saying they never do this, they always do that.

What I've written about their feeding is what I've found, in over 50 years of fishing all over the place, is true far more often than not. There are always the exceptions, and I shouldn't like anyone to think that because perhaps the water is only 35°F (2°C), or because the sun is shining brilliantly and the water looks like glass, that he ought to pack up and go home. I'm not the only angler who has found that sometimes, on what seems a hopeless day, you get just one bite — and catch a fish you'll remember all your life. Many a record fish has been the only one taken by its captor that day.

I think that a true angler should never be unhappy because

conditions are such that the chances of catching anything are poor. After all, we don't want the fish — when we catch them, we only put them back, unless of course they are good to eat, like salmon, trout or eels.

What we want is the pleasure of succeeding in overcoming the difficulty of catching them — and bad conditions only increase the difficulty of the problem.